BRITISH COLUMBIA BIZARRE

BRITISH COLUMBIA
Bizarre

Stories, Whimsies, Facts, and a Few Outright Lies
from Canada's Wacky West Coast

ROSEMARY NEERING

Copyright © 2011 Rosemary Neering

All rights reserved. No part of this publication may be reproduced, stored in a retrieval system, or transmitted in any form or by any means—electronic, mechanical, recording, or otherwise—without the prior written consent of the publisher or a licence from The Canadian Copyright Licensing Agency (ACCESS Copyright). For a copyright licence, visit www.accesscopyright.ca.

TouchWood Editions
www.touchwoodeditions.com

LIBRARY AND ARCHIVES CANADA CATALOGUING IN PUBLICATION

Neering, Rosemary, 1945–
British Columbia bizarre: stories, whimsies, facts, and a few outright lies from Canada's wacky West Coast / Rosemary Neering.

Includes bibliographical references and index.
Print format: ISBN 978-1-926741-25-3
Electronic monograph in PDF format: ISBN 978-1-926741-30-7
Electronic monograph in HTML format: ISBN 978-1-926741-31-4

1. British Columbia—Miscellanea. I. Title.

FC3811.6.N46 2011   971.1   C2010-907083-6

Editor: Marlyn Horsdal
Proofreader: Holland Gidney
Design, cover image, and interior illustrations: Pete Kohut
Author photo: Gary Green

We gratefully acknowledge the financial support for our publishing activities from the Government of Canada through the Canada Book Fund, Canada Council for the Arts, and the province of British Columbia through the British Columbia Arts Council and the Book Publishing Tax Credit.

The interior pages of this book have been printed on 100% post-consumer recycled paper, processed chlorine free, and printed with vegetable-based inks.

1 2 3 4 5 14 13 12 11

PRINTED IN CANADA

This book is dedicated to those who have created the quixotic, the unusual, the highly insignificant and the frequently ignored byways of British Columbia's history. It is for lovers of the weird, the wonderful and the wild.

May our tribe increase.

CONTENTS

Introduction ➤➤ 1
Highwaymen and Walking Whales, Anarchists and Opium

Chapter One ➤➤ 5
Anarchists, Bawdy Houses, Bullets, Buttocks and Bears

Chapter Two ➤➤ 29
Camels, Communists, Duels and Desperados

Chapter Three ➤➤ 55
Elephants, Editors and Flim-Flam Men

Chapter Four ➤➤ 89
Hangmen, Highwaymen, Horses and Hens

Chapter Five ➤➤ 111
Loathsome, Lulu, Madness and Moose

Chapter Six ➤➤ 135
Necromancers, Opium Smugglers and Not Dead Yet

Chapter Seven ➤➤ 149
Pigs, Potatoes and Pills for All Ills

Chapter Eight ➤➤ 169
Sea Serpents, Suicides and Theatre in the Wilds

Chapter Nine ➤➤ 195
Witchers, Wolverines and Want of Women

Endnotes 221 Bibliography 225 Index 226
Acknowledgments 231 About the author 232

⇢ Introduction ⇠

HIGHWAYMEN AND WALKING WHALES, ANARCHISTS AND OPIUM

In an era when non-fiction books are increasingly deep and narrow, this book is unabashedly shallow and wide. In it, you will find a plethora of amusing, unusual and sometimes shocking tidbits from the history of British Columbia. Amazing truths share space with falsities and fables, for sometimes in this province's past, it's happily difficult to tell fact from fiction.

This is not a balanced, nuanced history of BC that chronicles the important events, people and trends that formed this region. Instead, this book is unapologetically superficial, a tribute to the often strange, sometimes wonderful, and frequently insignificant, events and people that give colour to life in the past. It has virtually no socially redeeming value. It makes no claim to gender, race or age balance. With luck, it is equally unfair to everyone.

It takes advantage of the fact that this land on the western edge of Canada has been home to more than its share of losers, amusers and boozers. BC history is filled with odd tales, eccentric characters and outlandish schemes. Where else would a highwayman, insulted by newspaper coverage of his daring deed, write in with his own account (see *Highwaymen*, page 95)? And where else would a band of anarchists set up shop on a lonely island to create counterfeit currency with the help of dog hair (see *Anarchist Counterfeiters*, page 8)?

No story exists, of course, without the teller, and BC has been blessed in its story tellers. Throughout its history, newspaper editors as characterful as the people they wrote about have chronicled the happenings in their towns. Where else would you find a Colonel Lowery, five feet tall, lifelong bachelor, heavy drinker, and possessor of a vocabulary that outdid the dictionary, writing about a hockey game in almost Shakespearean terms (see *Hockey, Sort of*, page 99)? And when it comes to hyperbole, no one could outdo Ma Murray, legendary editor of the Cariboo and the Alaska Highway (see *That's fer Damshur*, page 187). Yet even the most serious of newspaper editors found time and space in their columns to retail more than politics and finance whenever they were amused or astonished by the antics in their towns. And writers from outside the region were drawn to the romance of the west, recording with apparent credulity every tall tale they were told and adding a few of their own invention.

Outsiders could scarcely be blamed for thinking BC the most colourful and bizarre of territories, for when news of the province was reported east of the Rockies or south of the border, it was most often the weird or wacky, not the sober and significant, that made the front page. If you read the columns of the *New York Times* a century and more ago, you would be convinced the region was filled with voracious bears (see *Bear Talk III*, page 20), whales that walked on land (see *Whale of a Tale*, page 209) and heinous opium smugglers whose tentacles reached from Victoria all along the American border (see *Not Just BC Bud, Eh?*, page 144).

This book has been a long-time project of mine. Often, when I was talking to an old-timer or looking in newspapers or government records or diaries for information for a book I was writing, I would come across a different story or whimsy that—irrelevant to my then current project—was too good to be ignored. A hermit to be disinterred because someone thought he might have had gold in his pockets when his rotting corpse was buried? An old-time prospector, severely hungover and with egg on his tie, waxing lyrical over breakfast in a Wells café about his memories of Cold-Ass Marie? Into the "Who'd a thunk it?" file they went, to be brought out as this book took shape.

They and the many other pieces in this book are my own personal choice for a portrait of *British Columbia Bizarre*. I hope they entertain you, make you laugh—and maybe even occasionally, provide some food for thought.

And a note on spelling and other sundries: to keep the flavour of the times, I have made no corrections to the way words are spelled, or to grammar, or to punctuation in direct quotes from historical sources; they are the way they are, inconsistencies and all.

Chapter One
Anarchists, Bawdy Houses, Bullets, Buttocks and Bears

ABDUCTION

What caught the attention of story tellers back in British Columbia's history? The same things that catch their attention now: the obscure and unusual, the unexpected and the exotic. Not surprisingly, accounts of crime and punishment were big in the newspapers, but it wasn't always the bloody murder or the massive embezzlement that caught the editor's eye. Sometimes, it was a gentler, more romantic story—though a strong theme ran through many such tales, of the hapless male entrapped by the helpless or scheming female, and relegated to the back porch of marriage for the rest of his life. From the Victoria *Daily British Colonist*, August 31, 1861:

> William Burns, a Kanaka, employed as groom at Dr. James's stables, was arrested on Thursday night charged with abducting a young countrywoman from the control of her guardian. Yesterday a private examination was had in the magistrate's office, which the lady, her guardian, and Burns attended, and after a short conference Burns agreed to marry the girl this morning at 11 o'clock, provided he was liberated. Some citizen went his security, and he departed with his intended clinging to his arm, looking as happy and contented as it is possible for a man who has had his head placed in the matrimonial noose without his consent.

AMAZONIA

Wrestling and prizefighting? Bring it on! Savage actions in the ring by brawny males, or even fights between men out behind the barn? Yes, indeed. But women battling women? Now there was an amazing sight.

On August 21, 1884, the Yale correspondent for the Kamloops *Inland Sentinel* reported on events in his town:

A few evenings ago, those who reside on Front street witnessed a contest the likes of which had never occurred in the previous history of our city. It seems that two of the Yale Amazons have had rather pugnacious feelings towards each other for some time, and happening to be at dinner at the 'Palace Restaurant' that evening, they concluded to settle the matter in dispute by a regular pugilistic encounter. Accordingly they repaired to the street, closely followed by the gallant proprietor who upon appearing on the scene, was immediately chosen referee. The preliminaries being duly arranged the battle commenced in dead earnest. The first four rounds were fought 'Sullivan style,' but not by Marquis of Queensbury rules. On the fifth round the muscles of one not being properly developed, and being considerably smaller than her opponent, she decided to resort to cannibalism, and forthwith surrounded her antagonist's biceps muscle with her incisors, but those present not wanting to see either of them come to an untimely end as this portended, just then interfered and stopped the show. Then for a time their delicate voices resounded musically on the night air, as each endeavored to explain the character of the other to the on-lookers, but finally becoming exhausted, quietness reigned once more. With the exception of the loss of a few handfuls of hair, and the tracing of some irrigating furrows, criss-cross over their noble brows, which time and the paint brush may eventually efface, neither party was badly hurt. The next morning the larger one started to find happier hunting grounds in the sunny south where the grapevine and the grasshopper flourisheth, and amazons are made happy by having everything their own way.

ANARCHIST COUNTERFEITERS

It's a long road from a university in Russia to a cramped cell at Leavenworth prison in the American Midwest, particularly when that road goes by way of a wooden house on Nootka Island, off the west coast of Vancouver Island. Throw in anarchists, country-wide searches and counterfeit money made by using hair from a dog, and you have one of BC's more unusual stories.

Albert Leon roused no public comment when he arrived in BC from Los Angeles in 1910, several years after he had fled Russia, apparently because of his anarchist beliefs and political activities. He bought a two-storey house on Nootka Island, near the native village there. He was described as twenty-eight or twenty-nine years old, of middle height and "prepossessing looking." He apparently was accompanied or soon followed by several other men, and told another resident of the island that he was setting up a colony of Russian anarchists. Perhaps they were among the coterie of Russian anarchists, enthusiastic and violent revolutionaries, who were jailed, exiled or committed suicide rather than be imprisoned around 1907.

Leon left the island shortly thereafter. In October of 1911, he was arrested in New York, on the verge of boarding a boat for British Guiana, and charged with counterfeiting thousands of dollars' worth of banknotes issued by a dozen American banks. (Until 1913, American national banks were authorized to issue their own banknotes, which by law had to be accepted by all other national banks.)

"Gang on Lonely Isle Ran a Money Mill," declared the *New York Times*. "Alleged Leader Arrested Here After Two are Captured in Chicago by Secret Service Men, Countrywide Search Ends, Country Flooded with Fine Imitation of $10 Bills, Made by a Secret Photographic Process, It Is Said . . .

"Working in a little shack in Nootka Island, British Columbia, the prisoner, they allege, perfected a system of photographing notes so his prints would pass without question as genuine."[1] Later reports suggested that Leon and his assistants had somehow used hair from a dog to achieve the "thread" effect that made the bills such good copies.

The Victoria *Daily Colonist* took up the story. "Vancouver Island has lost from among its residents of many diverse nationalities a genius whose ability to manufacture spurious currency has successfully been pitted against the shrewdest of American bank cashiers," the newspaper reported.[2] Some time later, a further story appeared, documenting the work of United States secret service agent W.A. Glover, who had voyaged to Nootka and brought back Leon's counterfeiting outfit.

According to the newspaper, Glover had found four Russian anarchists on Nootka, the remains of Leon's proposed counterfeiting colony, who intended to raise funds for revolution in Russia. He was told that ten other Russians were on their way to the island, still ignorant of their leader's arrest.

"They told Glover . . . that no more counterfeiting would be done by them. All of them were highly informed, plentifully supplied with money and writers of revolutionary propaganda. They declared that they had fled from Russia to escape prison or exile to Siberia, and that Leon had preceded them."

Glover reported that Leon had built a cabin, dug a garden and cleared a little land. In the cabin, he had built a darkroom for his photographic process, "which was pronounced by the secret service men to be almost perfect." When he left the island, he hid his equipment in a ravine, marking the hiding place on a chart; the government man found the chart, but had difficulty locating the cache. "Had not Glover pushed his stick into a bundle of leaves at the foot of an immense tree, and struck the trunk, it would probably never have been located."[3]

When he was arrested in New York, Leon told police he had been in Kansas City, buying angora goats. He was offered a meal before being locked up, but refused, saying he was a vegetarian, and "I only eat at stated periods."

Though he at first denied any connection to the counterfeiting ring, he and two confederates eventually pled guilty and were convicted. Leon and Rudolph Swanson were sentenced to ten years each, Fred Marneek to five.

Transported to Leavenworth, Leon set to work using his undoubted artistic talent, and created what was termed "the most famous piece of work ever done at the institution." Titled *This Man Welcomes Sinners and Eats with Them*, a quote from the gospel of St. Luke, the large oval picture for the prison chapel was, apparently, made from old bedsheets and leftover construction materials. It was featured in various magazines in the 1920s and 1930s, but was destroyed in a prison riot in 1992.

And what of Leon after he was released from Leavenworth? His name does not appear in the news columns again; he seems to have slipped into obscurity.

ANIMAL ANTICS

There was something immensely appealing about the wild side of BC. Newspapers as far afield as the *New York Times* and the Toronto *Globe* loved nothing better than a good story about bears—though cougars (sometimes known as panthers), wolves and even raccoons were a sure thing for the lighter side of the news. Man-meets-beast, woman-beats-beast—and, if they could get it, beast-eats-man—reinforced the image of this province as the really wild west, filled with primeval danger. From the *New York Times*, November 7, 1898:

> Bears and cougars, impelled by the pangs of hunger, are invading many towns in British Columbia and are terrifying the ranchmen. Four bears entered White Water City, in Kootenai, recently at night, attacked the meat safe of the principal hotel, demolished it, and got away in safety with its contents. The entire male population turned out the next night, armed with rifles and shotguns, and awaited the advent of the bears. Soon after midnight the bears arrived and a terrific fusillade ensued. When the smoke had cleared away it was discovered that two of the four had fallen. Nanaimo, also, was visited by bears, and the women and children had a scare. One panther waited all night in the branches of a tree overhanging the ranch house of Mrs. Dunster. She shot him dead next morning.
>
> Mrs. McEnnery, while acting as a nurse in a wealthy farmer's house, saw a cougar peering through the

window at her in the moonlight. She seized the boy and rushed from the back door to a neighbor's house. On the neighbor returning, the cougar was found to have entered the shed. He was shot dead from the open door of the dining room.

ARSON, ETC.

An account of the day in court appeared frequently in newspapers. There's nothing like the roster of cases heard by a magistrate to paint a picture of the side of town life that respectable burghers would rather keep quiet. Arson, insults, failure to support a spouse and youthful hijinks kept readers amused or annoyed in 1897 Victoria, where the newspaper carried a long report of the day in court and the assorted cases that were heard. From the Victoria *Daily Colonist*, September 10, 1897:

> Youthful depravity and unneighborly quarrels constituted the underlying cause for the major portion of the grist of cases which Police Magistrate Macrae had before him yesterday, and which kept the court in sessions all the morning and afternoon. There were one or two more serious cases, the most important being a charge of arson made against a miserably clad woman named Ellen Burns, who appeared in the box with a crying baby in her arms. Ellen is alleged to have had a "grudge" against a neighbor on Discovery street, and when this neighbor Catherine Dickinson, had, thanks to the gentleness of the Magistrate, overcome the disposition to garrulity which is characteristic of so many of the fair sex when they get into court, she testified to certain language having been

used by the gentle Ellen which altogether debars that individual from any claim to being numbered amongst those to whom the name lady can be applied. But Ellen did worse than this it is alleged, for under the cover of darkness she was observed by no fewer than three eye-witnesses to make three mysterious visits to the house occupied by Mrs. Dickinson, carrying in her hand on two of the said visits a can, the contents of which are surmised to have been coal oil, a supposition which is based upon the fact that a very few minutes after her third and last visit to the place, a passer by noticed that fire had broken out on the exterior of the building, Fortunately the flames were discovered in time for them to be easily extinguished by the employment of three or four buckets of water, but the odor of coal oil was sufficiently pronounced to make itself apparent to those who put out the fire . . .

Francis Ellis, who apparently desires to enjoy the felicities of marriage without the consequent disadvantages in the matter of expense, was charged with vagrancy and failure to support her whom five years ago he vowed to love, honor and cherish. Five dollars in three months is surely inadequate for the support of the most modest menage, and little surprise can be expressed at the fact that Mrs. Ellis had to raise $24 on her own credit to keep the little house intact from the threatened invasion of the sheriff. Francis Ellis will appear on Tuesday to explain his conduct or suffer the penalty.

A trio of small boys who have been making things very unpleasant for Mr. N. Pointer by indulging in language which should be as Greek to those of their tender years, were kept all day on short commons, and although the evidence adduced was only considered sufficient to convict one of the three offenders, and although all were discharged, the lesson they have learned will no doubt prove sufficient to deter them from a course of action which, intended only for the annoyance of their victim, has resulted in the administration of a useful lesson to the tormentors.

ASTONISHING FEATS

From the Victoria *Daily British Colonist*, May 16, 1871:

Cook has again performed the 'astonishing' feat of sitting in a tub to which were tied, limb and wing, 4 unfortunate geese, and floating placidly with the current of a stream. The affair is called a 'goose-race,' but whether the title is most applicable to members of the human race who assembled, or to the injured birds, we leave those who witnessed the race at the Gorge to decide.

AUTO FROLICS

When the first automobile—a huffing and puffing Stanley Steamer, driven by a steam boiler—took to BC streets in 1898, the battle between the horse and the car was launched. And that's not necessarily a metaphorical term: often the battle was physical, with cars running into horses or horses running panicked from cars. The rickety streets of a newborn Prince Rupert were the scene of one such debacle. From the Prince Rupert *Daily News*, May 2, 1911:

The noise of the only auto in Prince Rupert yesterday afternoon terrified a team left unwatched at the top of Third avenue. One horse was hurt so badly by the impact when the team brought up against a rock pile that it had to be shot. F. Kelly of the Union Transfer Co., owner of the horse wrote last night to the council to have something done about the auto. It was proposed to refer the matter to the Chief of Police. This was Alderman Newton's suggestion. Alderman Morrissey was strong for the protection of women and children at risk from runaways considering the condition of the streets. All the blame was not attached to the auto by Alderman Smith who knew that the team had been unwatched and untethered... The Chief of Police is to warn the owner of the auto, and to get after the owners of teams and drivers to have their horses watched or properly weighted when left.

BAGATELLES

Wiggs O'Neill, raconteur extraordinary of early white men's days on the Skeena River, tells about a native woman who visited the railway construction camps in Kitselas Canyon on the Skeena around 1911. As Wiggs put it, she was "putting the gangs on a spree and disorganizing the crews." The area constable raided the camps and brought the woman back for trial. The charge was read, but the woman said nothing. Questioned in English, Chinook, Cree, pidgin English and Blackfoot, she responded not a word. Well, they thought, she is either deaf and dumb or not very bright. So the Justices of the Peace fined her $25. She took a knotted handkerchief out of her pocket, undid a few knots, and peeled two tens and a five from a big bankroll. "Thanks, Gentlemen," she said, "it was a mere bagatelle," and strolled from the room. Later, someone revealed she had graduated from one of the area's mission schools.[4]

BAGNIOS, BAWDY HOUSES AND BROTHELS

There was one in every town, or two or three or more. Call it a brothel, bawdy house or *bagnio*, it presented, from one point of view, a necessary release or reprieve from loneliness. From the more censorious point of view, it was a disgrace, to be railed against from pulpit and editorial page. Though they pretended ignorance, everyone in a small town knew perfectly well what went on in those houses. Once in a while, an honest newspaper editor even admitted he was personally aware of the activities he condemned.

The soiled doves and sporting girls, as they were called, were usually housed in brothels grouped together at some distance from the respectable part of town, at the end of "Main Street" or in a separate district. In towns where men were the majority—every mining-rush town, for example—a visit to the *bagnio* was for more than sex: it also promised an evening with alcohol, gambling and, if the men chose well, some music and dancing. Long after the fact, a prospector who spent the Depression years in Wells, in the Cariboo, reminisced every time he was in his cups about the aptly nicknamed Cold-Ass Marie and her housemates, and the lovely times the men of the town had had with them. In Sandon, an avalanche rolled down the mountainside and buried one brothel. The men of the town dug out the house, and it was remarked that quite a number of seemingly respectable men knew exactly where the madam's bedroom was.

Events at the brothels and the battles between the various madams and ladies were often reported, though in dressed-up euphemisms that didn't fool the smallest child. The *Daily Colonist* reported on December 15, 1900, that "there was a little celebration among the residents of lower

Chatham street yesterday, after the women who had been fined in police court returned to their homes. As a result, Daisy William is nursing a badly cut and bruised forehead, and Julia Moore is in the city lockup on a charge of assault. Daisy says Julia struck her over the head with a beer bottle, and showed the cut and produced the remnants of a bottle to prove that there was some force behind the blow."

In the winter of 1938, heavy rains in Zeballos "threatened serious consequences to the place known as the Goat Ranch.

"Situated nearly a mile from town at the low point where the river floods, it was half under water when the occupants were rescued by boats rushed by truck from the beach," reported the Zeballos *Miner* on December 12.

"The heavy rain reached its worst at night. Melting snow in the hills formed cascades down the steep mountain sides, swelling the Zeballos River to overflowing.

"Occupants of the Goat Ranch awakened when their beds began to float."

The storm tore down trees, flooded homes and threw a logging train into the Franklin River; logs tossed into the main street of Zeballos blocked traffic. The building that housed the Goat Ranch is said to have ended up as a loggers' bunkhouse on Zeballos Arm.

BEAR TALK I

Bears loomed large in the BC imagination. To read the big-city papers, you would think the forests were filled with rampaging black bears and not a few grizzlies. No story evoked more interest than hand-to-hand combat between a settler and a bear. In small-town BC, though, violent bear attacks were not half as much fun as—and much rarer than—the horse-laugh stories wherein a local was bested by a beast or mistook a domestic animal for a bear. From the Skeena *District News* in March of 1904:

> Sam Pearse, a citizen very well known, was loitering about in an aimless fashion in the woods to the rear of the town. Suddenly the dog, that accompanied him, set up a furious barking. Mr. Pearse investigated. The dog was at the mouth of what was, without doubt, a bear's den, and if further proof of that fact was necessary, it was supplied by the constant issuance from the den of stentorous snorts such as only Bruin is capable of making. Mr. Pearse, conscious of his imminent danger, fled, first having turned pale. He did not cease running 'til he had reached town ... It was promptly decided ... to call out for purposes of general defense and attack, such of the able-bodied citizens as were possessed of, or could borrow, fire arms. It took only a short time to marshal a phalanx of determined and blood thirsty looking men ... Half an hour later the army was cautiously approaching the enemy. The General cried "Halt!" and for a moment pondered as to whether a bold frontal attack should be made but ... decided that a wide flanking movement so as to turn, if possible, the enemy's

left ear and thus enfilade him in his den would be the safest. At this moment the enemy debouched into open view. Whereupon Mr. Pearse took cover and thoughtfully besought the rest to follow his example. When George Frizzell uttered a piercing shriek and said, "Why I'm cogswoggled if it isn't my cub Bruno that escaped from me last fall!" The excitement in the army then subsided and those who had begun a precipitous retreat, returned emboldened. Bruno shimmied up a tree and George dauntlessly shimmied after him. They went as high up as they could get and it was a small tree and the cub got out on a limb. George got opposite him and tried to wheedle him with pet names uttered in dulcet tones, but Bruno resisted these blandishments and would not "come." Then George drew from his pocket, which is usually stored with toothsome articles, a large rosy apple. This proved a fetcher and when Bruno shot his nose forward, he was seized by the scruff of the neck and hauled forward. Then began a battle royal between George and the cub. It lasted quite a while, neither participant apparently having the advantage, when at last the limb broke and bear and man in a firm embrace came crashing down through the branches and landed in the deep snow beneath. Neither was injured and George lifted his prey bodily and started home with him.

BEAR TALK II

The Bella Coola *Courier* reports another Stupid Tourist Question on May 13, 1913:

Our tourist finds, a little further on in the wood, a camp of several smoke-blackened, weather-scarred tents, an Indian woman cooking over a little fire; two dark men scraping flesh scraps from a fresh bear-hide, throwing these to a dog.

'How old?' queries our tourist.

'Dunno; bear not tell me when I shoot 'um.'

BEAR TALK III

From the Prince Rupert *Daily News*, May 10, 1911:

The settlers around Massett are quietly retailing a story at the expense of one of their number who shall be nameless. He had been very anxious to land a bear, and visions of juicy bear steaks and a beautiful black fur robe rose before him when he heard a scrambling in the thicket a few days ago.

Carefully loading his gun, and creeping out into the bush he went to get Mr. Bruin. Cautiously creeping around tree stumps he got nearer and nearer to the sounds. Then he rose rifle in hand just as a great black bear about the size of the east wall of a house rose at him.

He took no chances. Bringing his gun into play he let fly right into the heart of the mass. When the sounds of the dying animal's squeals and groans had subsided, and he knew the animal was dead, he went up to examine his prize and found—a neighbor's pig. There is mourning in the neighboring pig stye now, and subdued laughter wherever two or three of the settlers are gathered together.

BEAR TALK IV

There were times, however, when an encounter between bear and man verged on the truly heroic, though perhaps as much on the outgunned bear's part as on the man's. Such a battle not far from Yale was reported first in the Emory *Sentinel* in July of 1880, then the story was picked up by the *New York Times* to run in great detail on page 5 of its August 15 edition. "A British Columbia bear story," headlined the *Times* breathlessly, "thrilling experiences of a father and son—a fight for life with an enormous and enraged brute."

According to the story, Alexander Embree and his son Walter were standing in a field at the father's farm near Emory when they saw their sheep running and behind them an enormous bear creeping towards their horses, which were feeding on the hillside. The son ran off for a gun and an axe; by the time he returned, the bear was ready to spring on one of the horses. Embree *père* fired the gun; the bear ran away, leaving bloody tracks behind him. The dog followed, with the men behind him. A mile up the steep track, the dog, as dogs will do, ran back towards the men with the bear on his tail.

"On standing still for a few moments the bear came within 40 feet, apparently raging mad. For a moment the dog checked him and Mr. Embree fired at what he supposed to be the back of his shoulder but it proved to be the beast's enormous head, and he only struck him on the lower jaw, breaking off a part of the lower jaw and one lower tusk and a part of the tusk on the other side, and that no doubt saved their lives. Mr. Embree instantly loaded again, but when the monster sprang upon him, the cap failed to explode. He used the gun over the brute's head, the second blow . . . appeared to produce no more effect than a riding whip in the hands of a child. At that point in the conflict the bear pushed hard upon his foe, when a log behind Mr. Embree tripped him, and he fell backward with the monster upon him. The bear was about taking Mr. Embree's head or face in his mouth when the latter thrust his right hand into the bear's mouth and caught his tongue, but unfortunately his arm coming out across the animal's mouth, the monster shut it upon the arm, and crushed both bones; in the man's own words, 'as easily as you would break a pipe stem.'"

The son hit the bear on the back of the head with his axe, but just cut him slightly. Further annoyed, the bear turned on the son, knocking the axe some ten metres away. He grabbed the son by the knee and shook him as a dog shakes a rat. The father, without weapons, jumped on the bear's back.

"Twice this dreadful game was played turnabout by father and son, each in his turn attacking the bear to save the other's life. While they were under the bear he held them down with his front feet, and tried to tear them with his hind heel, but it . . . only tore the earth under them. The final struggle was fearful. The bear had the young man underneath him and in an attempt to crush his head between his enormous jaws, for the want of the lower tusks he was only able to tear the flesh from his forehead down over his eyes, and holding the skin of his forehead and eyebrow in his front teeth, shook the young man violently. At this moment the old man caught sight of the axe, and taking it in his left hand, began to strike at the bear's head, the axe often coming close to his son's face in the deadly struggle, and after having given the brute ten blows with the axe from one hand, the bear released his hold from the son's face and fell, from a blow between his eye and his ear, dead, upon the bleeding body of the young man, who during the last struggle had held a firm grip of the bear's tongue.

"The father, with one finger bitten off and his right arm crushed, had to help his wounded son home, the latter having both knees fearfully mangled and his face bitten and torn."

The men were expected to recover, though they would not be able to work on the farm for a while. The bear was the largest the men had ever seen. "Never," wrote the reporter, "did father and show more pluck in defending each other from a fearful death." Neither paper commented on the bravery of the bear.

BIBULOSITY

A Port Essington magistrate identified only as Billy was rather fond of drink. One night after imbibing, he collapsed in front of the meat market. His companions commandeered a meat truck and wheeled him to his home at the top of a long flight of steps. They propped him up against the door and sang, "For He's a Jolly Good Fellow," falling silent only when Billy's wife flung open the door and knocked her husband over. Not long after, the local constable arrested the friends and dumped them in jail overnight. The next morning, they appeared in front of Magistrate Billy himself. He fined them each $50 and costs. "How could you do this to us?" they yowled profanely later as Billy passed them on the street. "That'll teach you to sing 'For He's a Jolly Good Fellow' to me on my doorstep at two in the morning," the magistrate muttered in return.[5]

BOOTIFUL

In *BC 1887, A Ramble in British Columbia*, W.J. Clutterbuck and J.A. Lees described their trip around the province, and poked fun at their companion, the footsore Cardie, a long, dark and good-looking young man who, they said, lived all alone in a log cabin 10,000 feet above sea level.

> As Cardie remarked: "This B.C. weather goes by fits and starts: it gave us fits yesterday and lets us start to-day." In spite of this flippancy, he was not on the whole very genial, owing to a slight misfortune. His boots being very wet had been hung up from one of the poles, to dry in the heat of the fire. Unluckily the high wind drove the rain all night in that direction, through the slightly open chimney, and in the morning when Cardie pulled on his first boot with a jerk, there was a splash and a fountain of water in all directions, and both of them were found to be about half full of rain.
>
> He was a little touchy all that day, especially when anyone "hoped his feet were not damp, because that would be dangerous in this climate," or made any similar kind inquiry; and some of his replies were conceived in the worst possible taste, and with an absence of gratitude that was positively sickening.

BULLDOGGED—ONE WAY OR ANOTHER

Bulldog Kelly aroused the wrath of editorialists across the province in 1884. The US refused an extradition request when Bulldog, who had fled to the US, was charged with murdering Baird, the bootlegger at Golden. "Although the evidence was conclusive," opined the *Daily*

Colonist, "through political influence Kelly was released, and a cold-blooded murder was unavenged."

Six years later, Bulldog was reported killed. Working as a train brakeman, he had slipped between cars, and both his legs were severed. Though still alive when picked up, he died in hospital. Thus started a legend and a treasure hunt, for Bulldog was reputed to have said he had lots of money secreted somewhere in Kootenay.

But the death story wasn't fitting enough for some. A chronicler by the name of Arthur Fenwick, renowned for his story-inventing ability, told it differently. According to Fenwick, Bulldog was living fine and high in Montana when a 13-year-old boy walked up and asked him if he was indeed Bulldog. "Yes," he said, "I am the great Bulldog." Whereupon the boy shot him, shouting that, three years earlier, Bulldog had killed his dad.[6]

BULLETS AND BUTTOCKS

From "The War Diary of the Prince Rupert Defences"[7]:

> A private of the Canadian Scottish at Barrett Fort accidentally fired his rifle, the bullet going through the walls of two huts, a bandolier, glass windows, folded blankets and finally lodging in the left buttock of Gunner Shelford.

BUTT I CAN'T MOVE

The attitude to malingerers, or supposed malingerers, in bygone days was rough and tough. No psychiatrists or medications, but a more direct trial to detect falsehood was applied to one man.

John Butts was well known in 1860s Victoria. An emigrant from Australia, via the goldfields of California, he frequently ended up in jail or on the chain gang, for supplying liquor to the native people, or selling stolen goods, or for being a rogue and a vagabond. He was also once charged with sodomy, the "commission of an abominable offence on the person of a little English boy," but that charge he escaped when the jury could not come to a unanimous verdict. He was for a time the town crier, in which position he shouted out not just the news and the hour, but vicious insults at a man he disliked. The man heard the words and caned Butts severely. The city wanted him sent away, but no ship's captain could be persuaded to let him on board. Butts said he would go willingly if only someone would give him the money for a ticket.

Butts finally left town on a ship sailing for China in 1866.

Presumably tired of the chain gang, he tried on one occasion to convince the authorities that he was paralyzed from the waist down, as reported in the Victoria *Daily British Colonist*, March 29, 1861:

> Our readers all know that the renowned John Butts was said to have been stricken with paralysis some six weeks ago, while an active member of the chain-gang, and was sent to the hospital in a hand-cart, where he was placed under the tender care of Dr. Trimble. Various means were adopted when he first entered the institution to find out if he was not humbugging; but every test applied, no matter how painful, was insufficient to induce him to use his feet. He persisted in saying that his legs, from his knees down, were paralysed. So the attendants finally gave over the application of tests, and suffered Mr. B. to recline upon a soft bed and read "religious" works—or on fine days to drag himself by means of his hands to the front stoop and bask in the rays of the sun. Yesterday, however, Dr. Trimble, while at the hospital observed a

suspicious movement on his part, which led him to suppose that the Colony was being swindled to the extent of his board. Immediately summoning all the able-bodied inmates, Butts was seized, stripped, and placed in a chair at the front of the house; eighteen buckets of cold salt water were obtained, taken to the top of the balcony, and thrown upon him from that height. Butts shivered and shook, but declared he could not budge an inch, although he begged the doctor to discontinue the treatment. It was no use. The doctor was inexorable. Eighteen more buckets of cold water were procured, and again poured over him. He shivered and shook considerably during the second bath, but would not rise. Again the attendants rushed for cold water—eighteen buckets brimful were arranged on the balcony, and the attendants commenced to shower them down on the supposed helpless creature. The impostor stood it pretty well until the contents of the ninth pail had reached him, when he suddenly jumped from the chair and slid out of the way. A burst of laughter arose from all present, and after the supply above had been exhausted, Butts emerged from his hiding place, leisurely pulled on his trousers, and then deliberately, in full sight of a dozen or more white persons, laid down on the grass and slowly dragged himself again into the hospital! It is now thought that John, having been a member of the chain-gang for three months for selling whisky to Indians, had adopted the ingenious device of pretending to be paralysed, in order that he might get over doing hard work, and purposed, when the ninety days were up, to quit the hospital and resume his old vocation. His fine times have been cut short, however, and notwithstanding he still persists in saying that he is paralysed, chances are that he will be sent back to work in a day or two. In case he refuses to move, we learn that the "water cure" will be resorted to again today. Much fun may be expected.

Chapter Two
Camels, Communists, Duels and Desperados

CAMEL LORE

Camels might seem unlikely beasts of burden for British Columbia, but where others saw insanity, packer Frank Laumeister saw opportunity. Camels had already been used in the United States in the ill-fated US Army Camel Corps; 34 camels arrived in Texas in 1856 and another 75 camels were shipped in 1857. The camels wore out their welcome, in, successively, the army, railway building, a camel freight train and the circus.

Undeterred, a San Francisco merchant arranged for 15—or 35—or some number in between—Bactrian camels from Manchuria and Mongolia to be brought from China—or from Russia (California camel reports are contradictory, as are the BC ones) in the late 1850s.

This worked out about as well as might have been predicted, and, in early 1862, two dozen of the beasts were advertised for sale in the Victoria *Daily British Colonist*. Laumeister and his partners took them on, despite the general hilarity that came with their imminent arrival. "Their greatest recommendation to Cariboo packers appears to lie in their long legs which will enable them to breast deep snowdrifts, the merest sight of which would disturb the equanimity of the strongest nerved or best conducted jackass in British Columbia," suggesting that next on the horizon were trained whales, which would carry freight and "inside passengers—a la Jonah" between Victoria and the Stikine.[1]

The camel owners got an extra when a baby was born soon after their arrival in Victoria. Mother and baby took to the wilds, perhaps impelled by the idiotic treatment meted out by one passerby, who dragged the baby around by the tail, and poked and kicked the mother. When the tormenter tried to pump the camel's head up and down, he paid for his actions: "with a noise resembling the rush of a full head of steam from a boiler, [she] forced through her nostrils about two gallons of dirty water."[2] The foolish and sodden man retired, vanquished. The mother and baby were seen here and there after their escape, and in November, were reported in the Cadboro Bay area. A few days later, a boy sent out to collect firewood was astonished and terrified to see two wild beasts bigger than horses, with humps on their backs. Both child and father, who went out to explore, reportedly returned "with blanched cheek and trembling steps."

The remaining camels were sent up the Fraser River by barge, then via the Lillooet route to the Cariboo. Alas, the beasts' tender feet were cut to shreds by rocks, their smell frightened other animals on the trail and fellow packers threatened to get rid of them if Laumeister would not. He persevered for some time, but finally gave in, and various camels were freed, or sold, or killed, or died in a blizzard, or were buried with a headboard to mark their fate, or given away, depending on the story you read. One survived long years at an Okanagan ranch; another was shot, supposedly mistaken for a grizzly bear, and served up as dinner at a hotel. "I have eaten many delicacies in my time . . . but for a never-to-be-forgotten dish, give me camel hump. I have often since regretted that the denizens of the Sahara desert have not acquired the art of canning."[3]

Whatever their fate, the camels were food for more than dinner: visiting writers told the story, taking fantasy for fact—or not much caring which was which.

"A curious story was told of a dromedary, which, with several of its brethren was once introduced into this country [the East Kootenay] by an enterprising packer in the early rush for gold," ran one such tale. "This genius having noticed that the ship of the desert was of a registered tonnage equal to about four mules, with hardly as much original sin as one, commenced a very profitable career with his novel pack-train. Unfortunately his fellow-packers conceived a prejudice against his invention, for the evident reason that if persisted in mules and horses would become a drug in the market. This prejudice they demonstrated by shooting at him and his dromedaries whenever they saw them, a course of action which speedily resulted in the survival of one, doubtless the fittest ... This wise beast thereupon took to its heels, and disappeared in the forest, and the packers had rest for many years.

"At the end of that time a hunter one day met an animal the like whereof he had never set eyes on, so grisly, grim and shaggy was its appearance, so humped its back and long its legs; but as it used these latter away from and not towards him, he pursued after it ... he shouted after it, 'Couchez cochon! Sacre nom d'un pipe! Morbleu!' and the other endearing epithets wherewith its defunct master, a French Canadian, was wont to caress it. And the strange creature lay down, waited for him to mount between its humps, and carried him triumphant to Tobacco Plains, where for many years it laboured as a beast of burden, and was finally eaten one day when people were hungry. It had provided itself in this cold climate with a coat of marvellous warmth, and was altogether so changed from its original appearance as to be practically a new development of species."[4]

According to historian Bruce Ramsey, said camel was turned loose after a time, and eventually shot for winter meat supply.

CAMP COFFEE

From *BC 1887, A Ramble in British Columbia*:

The very coffee in our cups froze before we had drunk more than half of it. This is a fact but possibly some caviller may be found to dispute it, and to ask why if we drank the first half before it froze, we did not drink the other half as well. To such we reply that it was too hot when first poured out.

CAMP COOK

From the Rossland *Miner*, September 9, 1899:

A firm in this city recently sent some beef to a lumber camp at Patterson and by return mail received the following complaint: Messrs. Blank & Co., Rossland—Gentlemen: The cook has complained that the beef you sent has no kidneys and little fat left. Perhaps it is all right, but she thinks an animal that could live without kidneys should have been on exhibition as a freak and not killed for the use of lumbermen. She tells the writer that there is a future in that brand of cattle for museum purposes, but she would much prefer the old style, and so, when shipping, to insure peace in this camp, send her the same sort as she knew in her girlhood days.

CAMP LIFE

Most of the time, small-town residents accepted the condescension sent their way from big-city folk, even if it came from Toronto. But sometimes, they fought back. Newspaper editor J.J. Langstaff was determined to show that the West Kootenay mining-rush town of Sandon was a pretty good place to be as reported in the *Paystreak*, January 16, 1897:

> It is really laughable the idea than many people entertain as to the desirability of Sandon as a place of residence. It is currently believed on the outside that the inhabitants of Sandon exist on pork and beans washed down with forty-rod of extreme potency, and that the sun never shines here. Now we would like to disabuse the good people of that belief. We do not deny that on some occasions the boys fill up on Slocan nerve tonic and want to eat a tenderfoot out of sheer exuberance of spirits, but the tenderfoot need not be eaten if his running powers approach anywhere near to the standard. We often vary the pork and beans diet by a little beef, and the forty rod with coffee and it is even asserted that quail on toast is not unknown on the bill of fare of our restaurants. Our citizens wear biled shirts on special occasions, and a plug hat fails to inspire them with sanguinary emotions. We have good whisky, better water and as pretty woman as there is in the country. We smoke good cigars, part our hair in the center and are regularly told to keep our feet on the sand and avoid Hades on Sundays by our religious pilot. We have ocular proof that there are spots on the sun and occasionally we have an opportunity of walking out with our best girls by the witching light of the moon. All these we have, and because we have more money than falls to the lot of the average man in other places, we do not think that the finger of scorn should be pointed at us, for we cannot help it. And if we could only get a Toronto man to

help us take care of some of it, our cup of happiness would be filled to overflowing.

CANADA, EH?

Being disgruntled about the federal government is a British Columbian's birthright. Threatening to secede is equally righteous—though sometimes, it's the north threatening to secede from BC or Pouce Coupe from the north. In 1885, British Columbians were aggrieved once more. The Toronto *Globe and Mail* reported on June 19, 1885:

> The intense feeling of dissatisfaction toward the Dominion Government's land tax is spreading throughout the mainland, and secession is openly threatened. A telegram was sent to Ottawa yesterday, which says that if an attempt is made to enforce the regulations there will be open rebellion. It is reported that men are arming in several districts, and a feeling of insecurity pervades official circles.

CAT STUFF

From the Zeballos *Miner*, August 29, 1938:

> Tommy, a black cat, is the self-appointed time keeper at the Central Zeballos mine. Morning and night he escorts the miners to work, walking up and down a distance of 2000 feet each way on a 4 inch iron air pipeline.
>
> Tommy takes his responsibilities very seriously, and when walking the pipe where it crosses the canyon at considerable height above the ground he attends strictly to business, looking neither to the right nor to the left.

CATALINE

The photos show a rough-looking dude with longish greasy hair, always in the same clothes—hat and waistcoat, baggy trousers and collared shirt. He looks like the kind of guy you'd like for a friend if you were in a tough spot and hate to have as an enemy. No one is quite sure where he came from, and few could understand exactly what he said. But he was a gentleman of a backwoods kind, good to the native people he worked with, and the best packer and mule skinner BC has ever seen.

Born in France near the Spanish border, Jean Jacques Caux arrived in BC in the early 1860s. Someone asked him if he came from Catalonia. Caux didn't understand the question but nodded anyway. Thence was born the name Cataline, and thus he was known until he died. In the 1860s and 1870s, he led his mule trains through the Cariboo. In the 1880s and 1890s, he freighted in the Omineca.

Stories about the legendary packer abound. He spoke a strange mixture of English, French, Spanish and a language all his own. Hazelton policeman Sperry Cline knew Cataline when the packer was in his eighties, and the two conversed in three languages at once, apparently with perfect understanding. He was all but illiterate, but had a formidable memory and his ability to calculate charges or payments was extraordinary.

He wore his trademark boiled shirt—a dress shirt boiled in starch—a new one put on at the beginning of every trip, heavy trousers, wide hat and silk neckerchief. When he traded with the native people, he added an elderly frock coat, greenish with age, and a French hat. He drank cognac—or brandy—or whatever he could get. He rubbed a few drops of each drink through his hair, declaring "a little inside, a little outside."

He led his 60-mule trains some 15 kilometres a day over mountain passes, through forests, along barely visible trails, to mining and construction camps. He travelled light, with little more luggage than a frying pan and a canvas to cover himself when he slept. He always carried a throwing knife; even when he was in his eighties, fools who thought it amusing to tease or challenge him were soon treated to a display of his throwing talents, and needed no more discouragement.

He could make a mule go when others failed. He could pack through snowstorms, rain, mud and any other condition that he found along the trail. If, perchance, his mules died of disease, exhaustion or misadventure, he still brought his goods through, on his own back or those of anyone he could hire. In an era when some packers treated their native helpers poorly, yet were surprised when mules or goods disappeared from their trains, Cataline treated his men well, and was known for rarely losing an animal or a pack.

Cataline led his last mule train in 1913, retiring when the railway reached Hazelton. He died in 1922, at the age of 93. He is buried in the Hazelton cemetery, where his grave looks out from the top of the cliff to the wide Skeena River flowing below.

CATTLE DRIVE

The Klondike gold rush of 1898 drew thousands of hopeful miners and merchants to the Yukon, and every one of them had to eat. Norman Lee, an Englishman ranching in the Chilcotin, looked northwards and saw an opportunity to make enough money to return to his beloved home country, where the wolves didn't howl at night and where you could walk paved streets instead of struggling through deep Chilcotin mud. If he could just drive 200 cattle to the Klondike, butcher them there and sell the beef, he would have enough money to buy a ticket home and more. He told his sister in a letter, though, that if the cattle drive did not pan out, he'd still get home—even if he had to steal a ticket.

He started out from his ranch and soon was on the telegraph trail. It wasn't lonely: he reported "all kinds and varieties of horses, all sorts and conditions of men . . . hung all over with six shooters and bowie knives," all presumably on their way to Klondike riches. One of Lee's men said he was sick; Lee thought he was pretending, but had to send him home when he swelled up all over and his face turned blue. Lee recorded he was "frequently so blind and dizzy with that grand American complaint 'Dispepsy' that I couldn't count the cattle properly."[5] But on they went, bookended by other pack trains, other cattle drivers, all with the Klondike on their minds.

One steer died of plant poisoning and others sickened, but "we heard afterwards that the proper course [to cure them] was to bleed them by chopping off a piece of their tails and feed them bacon grease." But by the time he learned of this remedy, they had long passed "poison place." Some two months into the drive, they arrived at Hazelton, on the Skeena River. The travellers ahead of them had turned the trail into a sea of mud; they threw away everything they could to lighten their loads—shovels, picks, a large tent, even the horses' hobbles.

As winter approached after five months on the trail, Lee was forced to butcher the herd. He loaded it onto scows on Teslin Lake. The scows foundered and the cargo was sunk; he made not a cent on his cattle drive. He and his one remaining man managed to get to Wrangell, Alaska, and return to Victoria by steamer.

Lee went back to his ranch. Four years later, he returned to England, where he married, then came back to the Chilcotin with his bride. He became one of the fixtures of the Chilcotin, his old store at Lee's Corners still open today.

COMMUNISTS—WELL, SORT OF

As early as the 1870s, critics were hurling the epithet of "Communist" at anyone who dared support some sort of socialism. In that year, the editor of the Victoria *Daily Colonist* railed at the editor of the short-lived Victoria *Standard*, which he termed "the Communist organ," for supporting something the *Daily Colonist* opposed. The *Standard* man was dubbed a Communist because he supported the Paris communards who took to the streets in the rebellious year of 1871, and was a man who shared views with Socialists, a group "whom every right thinking man must regard with horror and aversion—men steeped to the lips in the foulest crimes that can be committed by human instrumentality,"[6] skating over the fact that thousands of Communards had been lined up against a wall and shot after French government troops broke their two-month hold on the city.

BC, of course, was to see many more Communists, especially during the post-First-World-War and Depression years, when they were set to either tear down the machines of the state, or build up the lot of the working man—or both, depending on your point of view. Yet there was room for some humour amidst the epithets.

"Once the Victoria Press Club, to enliven its annual ball, hired a broken actor to make a Communist speech and if possible create a mild diversion," reported *Maclean's* magazine, on December 15, 1950. "He succeeded so well that the ballroom witnessed its first riot in which gentlemen broke one another's noses and women's gowns were torn off."

COOKS AND CASKETS

From the Victoria *Daily Colonist*, November 8, 1898:

> Robert Murray, cook of the [steamship] Comox, walked into Centre & Hanna's undertaking parlors last night, dazed from drink, and thinking he was on board ship, he pulled aside the curtain hanging before a casket and crawled into it for a sleep. He was discovered shortly after and taken to the police station.

COUGAR LADIES

Where there were cougars, there were cougar-killers, for BC settlers generally feared the wild cats and wanted them dead. The story of Ada Annie Rae Arthur, ornery west coast nursery owner, several times a widow—at least once under somewhat shady circumstances—and cougar-killer extraordinaire has been well documented. On the other side of the coast, in Sechelt, lived two other Cougar Ladies.

Minnie and Bergilot Solberg, brought by their parents from Norway in 1926 when they were small children, lived in the wilds of Sechelt Inlet almost all their lives. "Both women boasted hands like bear paws," read their obituary, "their skin thicker than sea-lion leather. Both were known for a 'little too much spittin' on the floor.'"[7] Both wore cowboy hats, thick sweaters and baggy jeans.

Described as a "mountain of a woman," Minnie lived up Jervis Inlet, perhaps for a few years with a husband—stories vary on whether she married or not, though she did have two children who were given up for adoption. Bergilot lived in an unheated shack, with neither electricity nor running water, on Sechelt Inlet. She flatly refused to move into town after her sister did so. She raised goats for milk and as a lure for cougars, wore a purple cowboy hat, and was never reluctant to voice her strong opinions: parks, for example, were bad places because you could neither hunt nor log in them.

Both sisters were fine shots, their skills attested to by the river-otter and cougar pelts they stretched outside their cabins. Both lived as trappers, hunters and guides. Both were famed for the stories they told, as well as for the lives they lived, interviewed by journalists from as far away as France. Minnie died in 2001, Bergilot in 2002.

COUNTERFEIT COINS

Some counterfeiters had noble motives and skilfully faked big bills (see *Anarchist Counterfeiters*, page 8), but others were both less political and less ambitious. In 1896, a man tried to buy five cents worth of notepaper in Nanaimo with a counterfeit dollar coin. Nope, said the store clerk, that's a fake. The man moved on, successfully buying himself a meal with the counterfeit coin, then paying for a drink with good money. The police chased after him and arrested him as he tried to board the boat for Vancouver. The fake coins, noted the *Daily Colonist*, were "of very inferior quality and ... easily detected."[8]

COW KILLING

On October 4, 1885, the *New York Times* reported:

> An accident has occurred on the Canadian Pacific Railway, near Kamloops, by which one white man and five Chinese were killed and a number wounded. A cow threw the engine from the track. The cars were badly wrecked.

CURSED CANADIANS

And again from the *New York Times* on November 10, 1899:

> The attention of the State Department at Washington has been called to the case of Mark Everett, an American miner, confined in the provincial jail at Kamloops, British Columbia, awaiting trial on a charge of stage robbery. It is alleged that Everett was kidnapped across the line from Republic, Washington, by Canadian officers. When within four miles of boundary, it is alleged, American officers overtook the party with the prisoner and attempted to serve a writ of habeas corpus, but were driven back by the Canadians at the points of revolvers and Everett was spirited to the other side during the hours of darkness.

DAMNING DEFENCE

From the police court news, Victoria *Daily British Colonist*, January 1, 1878:

James Good on remand, charged with stealing $22 from the Omineca Saloon.

After hearing six witnesses for the defence, all of whom strengthened the evidence against the prisoner, they each and all proving how he got the 75 cents found in his pocket, and their testimony entirely agreeing with that of John Stevens and others, His Honor sentenced the prisoner to 6 months' imprisonment with hard labor.

DEAD, REALLY DEAD

BC had a few pioneer bards worthy of the name, the most famous being Sawney, otherwise known as James Anderson, who wrote in Scottish dialect about the characters and events in gold-rush Barkerville. But there were others who put their rhyming minds to work, with results that varied wildly, for few versifiers could resist purple poetics and over-dramatization. One such was Crosbie Garstin, whose book, *Vagabond Verses*, was published in England in 1917. And yes, it seems that the subject of the poem was really, actually dead.

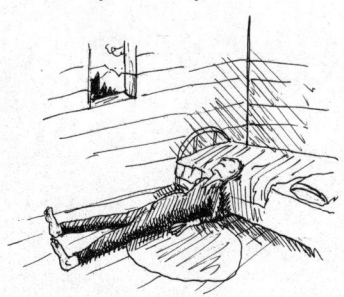

Dead! in his hut of rough-split shingles lying;
Two miners' candles spear the waving gloom.
Mourned by the mountain pines' wind-ruffled sighing
And thresh of rain without the barren room.

Its sense of peace and dreamless sleep despoiling,
A gash burns raw across the quiet head,
The black hair matted still with sweat of toiling
Dead!

Dead! and an end to him who heard the crying
Of scent-hot hounds across the dewy shires,
Who saw the golden dust of evening lying
On that fair city of the dreaming spires,
Who thrilled to violins and warmed the glances
Of gracious women, seized life, jewelled, red,
And flung, gay, gallant through her devil dances—
Dead!

Dead! and an end to all the bruised soul's tauntings,
To hells of memory that wake and blaze;
Dead, and an end to all the night-long hauntings
Of loves long lost and buried yesterdays:
An end to all the passion and the squandering
To loneliness, to squalor, to the dread
Of hopeless morrows, to the toiling and the wandering
Dead!

DEBT AND DEATH

What lengths might an indebted man go to? In 1881, the provincial legislature considered a private member's bill decreeing that, when an insolvent man died, the needs of his widow and dependent children could be put ahead of the rights of his creditors, and that a judge could order enough money set aside to support his dependents. The bill met with much criticism, since it might encourage a man to commit suicide, an act that would be unfair to his creditors. Presumably, it was acceptable for the man to shoot himself once he had paid his debts and left his family destitute. Reported the New Westminster *Mainland Guardian* on February 1, 1881:

> Mr. McGillivray considered that the clause would be a premium on dishonesty. A man might get into debt and then sit down and die in order that his estate might go to his wife and children.

The Victoria *Daily British Colonist* added on February 2, 1881:

> Mr. Wilson thought this was one of the most dishonest clauses ever inserted in a bill...A man could put a lot of property in his house and then shoot himself for the benefit of his family. A man's first duty was to pay his debts. A man may live in an extravagant way or his wife and family may live far beyond the means of their husband during his lifetime, may get a homestead and mortgage it and than when the husband and father died the whole estate was to be swallowed up to reward the family for having been extravagant.

DENTISTS

Even the dentist's office could make the paper on a slow news day. From the *Alaska Highway News*, March 8, 1945:

> Dr. Szilagy has been applying the forceps to many jaws this last week and some of our best friends are jostling with new dentures. Mrs. Powell of Charlie Lake took a day

off, went to the Hospital where Dr. S. removed a mouthful of good looking teeth which had gone wrong on her. W. Evenson was also a patient in the dentist's chair with a young jawful of teeth that had to be extracted.

DESPERADOS

The mythology of the Canadian west suggests that, unlike the American west, it was a law-abiding place, where a few stout lawmen kept the peace, and caused strong and desperate men to surrender quietly by the power of their demeanour and reputation alone. The reality was a little different. Highwaymen and murderers, thieves and rapists, men who committed despicable acts for gain, and those who committed them because they could, all walked the streets and rode the highways of the colony and then the province—and they weren't even all Americans. But a lot of them were pretty dumb (or drunk). One such appeared in Victoria *Daily Colonist*, on November 8, 1892:

Alexander Houston, the noted criminal and desperado who escaped from the penitentiary last March, where he was serving a 14 months' term for the murder and rape of an old Indian woman, aged 80, two years ago, was captured yesterday at Aldergrove. Houston has been spending the time since his escape in the mountains in Washington State, near Sumas City, and rode across the line on Saturday, proceeding to his father's house at Langley. Here he spent the night, and, after forcing his sister to give him money, cantered up to the village of Alder Grove. In the street of the village he met R. Shortreed and A. Murchison and, drawing a six-shooter, fired at the former, who retreated to the house, got guns and returned. Meantime Houston galloped to Shortreed's store, and tried to break in. Failing in this he mounted again and rode down the street flourishing a revolver and offering to kill anyone for $25. Shortreed overtook the desperado and called on him to surrender. Houston refused and raised his revolver, but Shortreed had him covered and fired a load of buckshot, killing the horse. Quick as a flash the outlaw was up, and Shortreed gave him the other barrel, severely wounding him. Houston then threw up his hands and surrendered. The officials here were notified and brought Houston back to the penitentiary.

The Victoria *Daily Colonist* recounts a battle that took place in Nelson, March 26, 1907.

Mannazino, the Italian desperado who shot his uncle at Kuskanook on Thursday and fled to the hills was captured last night after a desperate, but bloodless, battle.

A posse of police and citizens, under chief constable Bullock Webster surrounded him in his cabin in the mountains and it was feared that bloodshed would occur before he was taken.

The Italian's ammunition gave out after he had fired 100 shots, during a siege which lasted all Friday night and the better part of Saturday. Nobody was hurt.

1907 was a good—or bad—year for so-called desperados. "I'll blow all their blighted heads off when I get my Colts," the *Daily Colonist* reported a "bibulous gentleman" shouting as he rushed from a Government Street saloon. The mild-mannered desperado, as he was termed, aimed a rifle at two bar patrons and demanded their money or their lives. Nope, said the gentlemen at the bar. Neither. With that, the bartender grabbed the rifle, wrenched it away and threatened to hit the desperado over the head with it if he ever did that again, then ushered him to the door and threw him into the street. The bibulous one was not seen again.

And then there were the desperados from the early days on the Fraser, described in a letter to the magistrate at New Westminster in 1872:

> Two desperadoes made their appearance here yesterday with two boats laden with a lot of stuff apparently stolen from settlers along the coast—Constables Miller & Handy attempted to arrest them but they pointed the guns with which they were armed & the officers let them go. They were followed to English Bay last night where they left one of their boats in charge of the two Indian women who are with them. The boats were captured, after exchanging shots, & are now here but the men are at liberty & were last seen by the Indians at the Ranch on False Creek at 11 P.M. last night. The men are heavily armed, without jackets, one of them is fair about 5 ft 11 inches in height & supposed to be named Shipley &

worked for Moody about 5 years ago. The other is about 5 ft 7 and of dark complexion. The Indian women are both stout one of them is tall. Give notice at once to the settlers at the north Arm where they may go for provisions and to the police at New Westminster.

I have offered $50.00 for their capture which please justify my doing.

DIGITAL DOCKING

Canneries saw more than their share of accidents as the sharp knives came slicing down and salmon were packed into cans. Cannery workman Lew Hogan Jr. told canneries historian K. Mack Campbell about one such incident. Seems that Hogan was looking after the machines on the line at the Klemtu cannery. It was the job of a Chinese worker to keep salt in the salter, but the salt was always wet and plugging up in the salter. Hogan was accustomed to reaching down into the salter, tripping the lever and cleaning out the salt. The Chinese worker tried to emulate him, but things went wrong. "The next thing I knew, I see him holding his finger ... and I shut the line down because I didn't know what had happened. But there was no blood or anything and everything looked okay, so I started the line up again. And about half an hour later, the First Aid man was over there with some paper for me to sign. I said, 'What's this all about?' He said, 'We're going to have to send this man to town, to Vancouver. He cut his finger off.' I said, 'Where's the finger?' He said, 'I thought you had it.' So the only place it could be was in a can—sealed in the can."

They had been running through the day and had a lot of cans ready for packing. Should they open them all to look for the finger? Well, no. They called head office for advice. Head office said they had already sold that pack to China and the finger would just be going back home! They said, 'Let's just forget about it.' So we did."⁹

Every year, the company got cans sent back, because something foreign was inside. But the finger was never returned.

DOG DAYS

From the Aldermere, *Bulkley Pioneer*, April 10, 1908:

> "Mushers" under all kinds of circumstances are passing here daily bound for the new Eldorado on the Finlay River; single and in couples, and parties with back packs sleighs and toboggans without dogs and with dogs—collies, huskies, house dogs and all kinds of dogs, useful and useless. It is always Northwards Ho! Some are not very sanguine and when sore and lame lament the loss of the comforts of civilization, but mush on just the same.

DUELS

Duels to the death were not completely unknown in BC, but duels to the "well, let's just have a drink" were more common. Whether combatants were drunk, bad shots, or simply persuaded that dishonour was indeed better than death, few men were killed in BC duels.

Fort Kamloops chief trader Samuel Black, a volatile and aggressive employee of the Hudson's Bay Company, challenged botanist David Douglas to a duel that seems not to have taken place. But the most famous of the duels that didn't take place involved George Hunter Cary, the first attorney general of BC. Later to lose his job, his money and his mind, Cary was always eccentric. He was arrested once for galloping his horse across a bridge; his conduct was often unsuited to an attorney general. Soon after he arrived in the colony, he took issue with D.B. Ring of the *Daily Colonist* over whether Ring had called Cary a coward. Ring issued a challenge to a duel; Cary apparently accepted, but was then arrested. Why Ring was left free, the papers do not say. Cary was bound over to keep the peace, but declared instead he would rather go to jail. He did not, the duel was not fought, and matters seem to have settled down.

Some time after 1859, another duel was almost fought. Robert Stevenson was a prospector in the Okanagan whose horse was stolen. He armed himself with two revolvers and followed tracks to the Indian reserve. There, he found his horse and a native man, Ashnola John. We'll fight a duel, said Stevenson; march ten paces, turn and shoot to kill. Ashnola John evidently thought this was a dumb idea: when Stevenson turned, John had dashed well beyond revolver range.

In March of 1861, a saloon keeper and an unnamed colonel stood up against each other in Victoria's Beacon Hill Park. Both fired; the saloon keeper fell to the ground, blood flowing. The colonel stamped off, satisfied that he had killed his opponent honourably. Then the saloon keeper stood up, removed the sponge containing red ink that he had pressed to his chest, and walked away. Unlike the colonel, he had known all along that there was powder but no shot in the duelling pistols.

The non-duelling idea caught on. The Kamloops *Inland Sentinel* reported on March 26, 1883, on a near thing: "Yesterday [at Eagle Pass] a violent altercation . . . between Peter F. and a Ferryman, J.M., almost proved serious to one or both. A challenge had been given to meet in combat, and at the appointed time P.F. was on hand with a reliable shotgun, while the Ferryman put in his appearance with a patent revolver in hand.

"It so happened that Officer Todd, who had just arrived, got wind of what was going on and stepped upon the measured ground in good time to stop the dreadful deed about to take place. When Mr. Todd reached his hand for the revolver saying, 'I'll take the pistol, you take a sleep,' the danger was over. The heated blood has cooled and now peace is restored."

One duel did lead to death. In 1858, John Collins and "Tip the Boatman" William Morris got into an argument at the Beacon Hill cricket ground. Newspaperman and fact-embroiderer D.W. Higgins gives different names and a highly romantic account, but it's certain that Morris punched Collins, the requisite challenge was issued, the men met, paced out the requisite ten steps, turned, fired, and Collins was killed—apparently, though, on the third shot, which runs counter to the "one shot and we shake hands" etiquette of gentlemanly duelling. Morris fled to the US, where he got into trouble in a stagecoach holdup and murder.

DYNAMITE

From the Prince Rupert *News*, May 3, 1911:

> Havoc was wrought in the home of C.B. Wark on Third Avenue this morning by a heavy blast shot on Rick

Struga's station contract just behind the police station. A huge rock weighing over 600 pounds was flung high in the air and crashed down on Mr. Wark's house on the roof etc. rending its way through timbers and ceiling... just missing a handsome fauteil, cut through the thick carpet and buried itself in the floor. It took six men to get it out and the whole room was upset by the concussion... Other houses were fairly sprayed with spattered muskeg and smaller pieces of rock... Mr. Vernon W. Smith's house presents a mottled appearance owing chiefly to muskeg.

Chapter Three
Elephants, Editors and Flim-Flam Men

AN EARIE STORY

The *Kootenay Mail*, Revelstoke, talks about an incident in Salmon Arm, November 2, 1895:

> One of the most brutal and inhuman acts ever attempted in this locality was that of a man who has since left the settlement. Before going, he said he wished to bid goodbye to a neighbor here, and reaching out his hand the other took it. Then this individual grasped his other arm around his neighbor and bit off one of his ears. It was a most cowardly act as neither party was under the influence of liquor. The matter was settled out of court.

EARTHQUAKES

Earthquakes were rarely serious, but some reactions were cause for friendly teasing, and the quake itself could be the subject of some heavy-handed joshing and competition between communities. The Emory *Inland Sentinel* teased their neighbours at Yale on February 22, 1873:

> A number of snow slides have occurred near Yale recently, reminding parties of the rumbling sound that preceded the severe shock of an earthquake here, December '72 at

10 o'clock one moon-light night, when all nature was at ease and no foreboding indulged in respecting the end of the world or any lesser affair upon the banks of the Fraser; the people, however, felt alarmed and rushed into the streets, the bells rang from the vibration and dishes rattled upon the shelves, whole doors opened and shut without the use of St. Jacob's oil; even chickens flew off their roost and appeared to have the feathers, if not the nervous system, affected. After a few minutes the "fuss and feathers" was over and pale ladies and anxious gents again entered their lately deserted homes and otherwise; neither "cloud-capped towers or gorgeous palaces" had fallen at Yale, not a chicken had perished and the equilibrium of all parties in the burg was speedily restored and notes compared. The evening's entertainment summed up—no serious result.

The Portland Canal *News* was content on October 28, 1927:

Stewart experienced an earthquake last Monday morning at 8 o'clock or thereabouts, thus establishing herself in the status of the other great seaport of the Canadian Pacific coast, Vancouver, which bragged about her own individual earthquake until the question of a Pacific outlet for Peace River (which will be at Stewart) eclipsed the subterranean disturbance.

Those who were up felt a funny feeling. They saw the telephone poles waving about and had an idea they should send at once for Dr. Hillans. Some, in fact, experienced nausea and headaches. People in restaurants ran out in to the street and supplicated the sky when the coffee rambled out of their cups. Some clocks were stopped.

And Victoria was indeed amused—in parlance flowery and bombastic in the *Daily British Colonist* on October 10, 1863:

> We hear of bottles having fallen from shelves, crockery and plated ware striking up lively choruses, dogs barking, cocks crowing, and frightened citizens hastening out of doors regardless of personal appearances, to exclaim in the language of Bombastes— "What means all this?" —receiving the response echo— "Indeed, I hardly know!" But the most amusing effect which has come to our knowledge was the case of a well-known bachelor in this city who was slumbering in sweet repose, his dreamy imagination having probably wandered thousands of miles away and treasured up the recollections of some sweet form whose image was engraved upon that tablet which neither time nor separation could efface. Close by his bedstead hung a bag containing sundry articles destined at the end of the week to undergo an indispensable process at some Chinaman's laundry. The ruthless shock came, set the bag in motion, and caused it to touch the slumberer's shoulder. Starting up in his bed under the full conviction that he was a victim of foul play, our hero immediately betook himself to an Englishman's weapon of defence, and in the vulgar parlance of the prize ring, planted his right mauley with fearful vim upon the offending and helpless clothes' bag. On discovering his mistake, he muttered an apology and quietly nestled down again.

EDITORIAL FEUDS

Where was British Columbia's wild and woolly west? Where were the no-holds-barred battles? Occasionally in the saloons and the streets but definitely in the columns of the mining-town newspapers and even those of the big cities. Editors lashed out in wounding words or teased and made fun of their opponents and victims. Some were too wordy, some were maladept. But some created marvellous editorials and news columns that kept their subscribers reaching for each new day's diatribes.

Some were such great wordsmiths, their time at the helm of various newspapers so long, that they became well-known: Colonel Lowery of various Kootenay papers and "Ma" Murray of Lillooet and Dawson Creek are featured elsewhere in this book (*Lowery of the* Ledge, page 115 and *That's fer Damshur*, page 187). But they were not the only stars: others shone as well, though perhaps not quite as brightly, or for as long.

Until 1912, any team in the country could challenge the previous year's winner of the Stanley Cup to do battle, anywhere, anytime; frequently, a number of challenge matches were played throughout the year. Since its team had vanquished all the local competition, in 1911 the town of Phoenix, in the Boundary country, challenged the cup holders, the Quebec Bulldogs. The editor of the newspaper in neighbouring Trail dared to laugh at this idea. The editor of the Phoenix *Pioneer* let loose a barrage:

"The editor of the Saturday Sunset may be 'some pumpkins' in discussing gamblers, tinhorns, bootleggers and fourflushers, with whom he appears to be particularly intimate, but he is mighty small potatoes in discussing British Columbia hockey. He failed to take cognizance when Phoenix landed the three leading hockey trophies of the province, but gets busy with his little hammer when the challenge was sent to Ottawa."

The battle, unfortunately, was not played out in the rink. The Bulldogs sent their regrets, but they already had to face challenges from three other towns. They would be pleased to play three matches at the start of the following season, however, if Phoenix so wished. The idea died aborning.

Editors had harsh words for those who wanted things on the cheap. "The editor of the 'Islander' is of course working purely for his health, and for the good of the islands," wrote the man at the helm of the Queen Charlotte *Islander* in 1911. "Unfortunately, however, he has to eat, and would be arrested if he did not wear clothes. See the point? Two dollars, please."

The editor of the Portland Canal *News* took up the refrain on January 21, 1927. Annoyed by people who repeatedly asked him to bid on printing contracts but included all sorts of caveats, the editor asked what would happen if he did the same. "Suppose a printer should call up eight or ten different grocery stores and tell them to send a man down to give him a bid on a sack of potatoes, ten pounds of onions, and a can of pepper. Do you think they would do it?" He then penned a sarcastic riposte to a surgeon who wanted bids on different letterheads in various sizes, paper grades and colours, with the form left as is for possible future printing jobs.

"Am in the market for one operation for appendicitis, one, two or five-inch incision, with or without ether; also with or without nurse. Quotations must include putting appendix back and cancelling order if found sound. Successful bidder is expected to hold incision open for sixty days, as I expect to be in the market for an operation for gall stones, and I want to save the extra cost of cutting."

And sometimes the editor just suspended publication, because he could not obtain paper supplies or could not afford them, or because he was broke or bored or drunk. The editor of the McBride *Journal* did them all one better. "The Journal suspends publication with this issue," he wrote in April of 1917, in the midst of the First World War, "owing to the publisher having enlisted. It is hoped that if he is permitted to return safely to McBride, the issue of the paper may be recommenced."

EGGSEPTIONAL

From the *Alaska Highway News*, March 22, 1945:

> The old days of Fatty Arbuckle's pie eating marathons couldn't best Wynne "Scotty" Smith from Glasgow Toon who ordered two dozen soft fried eggs at the Pomeroy café last Monday and ate every one of them at one sitting. "Scotty" is a fine lump of man, youngish and handy with his fists. He has been mining coal at the King Gething mine and came into town to train up a bit for the boxing match that was scheduled to take place on March 17th. He worked up to the menu, by ordering half a dozen eggs, then a dozen and so on. He ate only the eggs, and swallowed them whole. Now that the boxing match is called off, Scotty has gone back to mulligans and Scotch broth.

ELEPHANT ESCAPADES

Forest fires had been burning for several weeks when the circus arrived in Cranbrook on August 6, 1926. Handlers began to unload the animals, including the 14 elephants that were the stars of the show. But something, perhaps the smoke in the air, frightened the elephants, and all 14 stampeded out of the railway yard and down Cranbrook's streets. How do you stop a stampeding elephant, let alone 14 of them? You don't. Within a short time, the big beasts had left town, and a message went out to railway crews on the CPR: "All trains east: Keep lookout for elephants on track."[1] Freedom was short-lived for seven elephants, recaptured within a day. Three more were discovered eating apples in an orchard. Several others were captured in a relatively short time. Charlie Ed and Myrtle—famed for her performance of the Charleston—were said to be travelling together. "[They] are fond of each other and almost jealous of each other," reported the Cranbrook *Herald* on September 2. "They've got lots to eat and drink up in the wilds and apparently take little jaunts of 30 miles to the mountains and then move on toward a creek for a drink."

But Myrtle had been shot several times, presumably by brave elephant hunters, was in poor physical shape and had pneumonia. When she was recaptured, those in charge decided she could not be saved and must be shot. A sad photo shows a man with his foot on the dead elephant, with the caption, "You are a good elephant now," presumably a lead-on from the thought, "The only good elephant is a dead elephant." Her skin was displayed in a Cranbrook shop window, her head and a foot sent to the University of Alberta, and her remains eaten by wild predators, including several grizzlies, one of which was shot near her mouldering carcass.

Charlie Ed was still on the loose. Born in the wild in 1910, captured and put to work doing tricks for circus patrons, he was a relatively small elephant. Almost six weeks after he escaped, he was sighted above Lumberton, some 20 kilometres away, in the hills southwest of Cranbrook. Ten elephant hunters mounted up and rode out of town, a posse committed to bringing Charlie Ed home.

For a day or so, they tracked Charlie Ed, finally catching up with him about seven kilometres from town. Circus spokesmen said he had recognized his trainer's voice, and docilely nibbled on bread until he was coaxed into capture. The newspaper, however, told a better story. Charlie Ed had no desire to return to captivity, even if it meant readily available food. Native Ktunaxa guides spotted the elephant, but when his keepers tried to fetter him, he knocked them down. The natives constructed a snare, faced the elephant and encouraged him to charge. He did—and ran into the waiting noose, anchored by two springy tamarack trees; the whip of the trees and the tightening noose did the rest.

The circus men hobbled Charlie Ed once he tired and brought him back to town. Two days later, the year's first snow fell on Cranbrook, weather that would presumably have given Charlie Ed problems.

To encourage locals to help out in the hunt, the circus men had promised that Charlie Ed would be a feature of the fall fair. He arrived back just in time; captured on September 15, he appeared at the fair from the 16th to the 18th. The newspaper reported the event: "At about 8:30 Charlie Ed. took his place on the sidewalk in front of the bank and in the presence of a number of citizens Mayor Roberts poured a bottle of real honest-to-goodness champagne over his head, at the same time declaring his name to be henceforth, 'Cranbrook Ed', instead of 'Charlie Ed.'"

Charlie Ed got a good breakfast at the arena, then a second one at a local café. He presented flowers to the winner of the "popular girl" contest after pretending to eat them. The circus paid $1,200 so he could have a baggage car to himself for his journey to California.

A happy ending? Maybe not. Ten years later, Cranbrook Ed was sold to a zoo; two years later, he turned on his keeper and trampled and shook him to death. He, in turn, was shot to death by police, at the age of 26.

EMBEZZLER

Hazel Wilby was an eye-catching woman, with a "physique that gave her distinction." And, indeed, she caught the eye of a Victoria press photographer as she walked through the lobby of Victoria's Empress Hotel in 1944. She was gone before he could snap a shot, but he reported back to the city desk, and the next day, a small item noted that the beauteous Hazel and her husband, Ralph, were staying at the venerable hotel on Victoria's Inner Harbour.

Ralph Wilby was actually on the lam from his former employers in New York, where, under a false name, he had embezzled all the cash he could get his hands on over a two-year period. He was, investigators had discovered, an ex-con who had served time and previously been deported from the United States back to Canada. Ralph had absconded with the cash, and it was thought that he was somewhere in Canada.

When someone in Ontario, aware of the hunt for Wilby, read the social note and passed it on, American detectives hastened to Victoria, where they lay in wait for the couple to return to the Empress. When they did, they arrested Ralph, and tried to ship him back to face charges of embezzling $386,921.29.

A Canadian citizen, Ralph demurred. Hazel retrieved some of the money that he had apparently buried somewhere near Victoria and paid a lawyer to fight extradition. Between writs, the detectives tried to get Ralph aboard a fishboat and bundle him back to the US, but Canadian officials stopped them and he was more formally extradited. He was then tried and convicted.

Facing a twenty-year sentence, Ralph asked for a deal. He told authorities he would reveal the whereabouts of the money if he could keep $10,000 for himself, money he said was actually his own. He had, he told his jailers, buried the money in the backyard of the Burnaby house where he and Hazel had been living. For three days and nights, police dug up the front, back and side yards of the house, finally finding some $225,000 buried a metre deep in tin cans. The Vancouver *Province* predicted he would get just a two-year sentence, free tickets to Africa for himself and Hazel, and $10,500 for rehabilitation. No such luck. He was sentenced to five to seven years in Sing Sing prison, with deportation back to Canada to follow. Hazel, apparently an innocent in the whole affair, divorced him, and they both had cause to regret that visit to sunny Victoria, as well as Hazel's amazing busty attractions.

Ralph Wilby was far from the only fugitive who thought he could successfully hide from American authorities in Canada. New York broker Adolph Israelowitz, for example, described after the fact as a youthful Russian adventurer, was accused of defrauding a number of businesses, individuals and relatives in 1917. Said the agents of the businesses, it's not the money—which came to about $25,000—but the principle of the thing: they wanted to make an example of him.

"For many days," reported the *New York Times* on November 10, "the detectives chased him from city to city through the West, and finally lost track of him altogether." But something in his papers led to a mysterious woman friend, with a fancy apartment, diamonds and a promise to marry, all furnished by Israelowitz. The woman suggested they look in Vancouver; Israelowitz was arrested in that city.

ESCAPE ARTISTS

Jails in infant mining towns were far from escape-proof. And if you found yourself incarcerated and without the proverbial file—though a hammer or axe would have been handier—your friends on the outside might help out. Once you were free, it was a short trip across the border to the US, whence you could be pretty sure that you would not be extradited, formally or otherwise, according to the Rossland *Miner* on August 31, 1899:

> Thomas Burns, who received a sentence of eighteen months at Nelson for robbing two bartenders at the circus canteen on the 18th of August, was evidently not favorably impressed with the surroundings at his new place of residence and seized the first opportunity to escape. The jail authorities at Nelson evidently kept the matter quiet, as nothing was heard in Rossland about the escape until today, when Constable Devitt of Trail, was ordered to go to Northport, where Burns was under arrest. The constable returned in the afternoon empty-handed, as the prisoner, having had one taste of Canadian justice, was in no way inclined to return for another dose, and declared he would fight extradition.
>
> The police anticipate no difficulty in securing the transfer of the fugitive to this side of the line, though there may be some delay.

The prisoner, in telling his experiences to the constable yesterday said, "The Rossland police are pretty slick all right, but those Nelson fellows are easy." From which it may be inferred that Mr. Burns has not been unacquainted with police methods in the past.

THE EVIL OF LOUNGING

From the Kamloops *Inland Sentinel*, September 11, 1884:

A writer on health very justly condemns lounging, which a very large number of persons indulge, as injurious to health. He says:—"An erect body attitude is of vastly more importance to health than is generally imagined. Crooked bodily positions, maintained for any length of time, are always injurious, whether in a sitting, standing or lying posture, whether sleeping or walking. To sit with the body leaning forward on the stomach or to one side with the heels elevated to a level with the head, is not only bad taste but exceedingly detrimental to health . . ."

EXPLOSIVE FASHION

With no Internet to publish urban myths, British Columbians had to depend on their newspapers to spread unfounded fears. In Prince Rupert during railway- and town-building days, careless handling of dynamite meant that residents really did have to be concerned about flying debris. But their newspaper editor was happy to add to their worries by exaggerating the explosive potential of nitrocellulose. Here's what the Prince Rupert *Daily News* had to say on May 20, 1911:

> [That] Prince Rupert girls who dread being hurt by a blast fired in the street-grading, and who go cautiously accordingly, may be the unsuspecting wearers of gun cotton ribbons and explosive waists liable to blow up at any moment, is a startling possibility just brought to light. Nor is the masculine sex immune from the danger since socks and ties may likewise be articles of destruction. This unsuspected condition of affairs has been discovered through a protest recently filed against the manufacture of artificial silk from cellulose, in which it appears there is a possibility that almost any article of wearing apparel made to imitate real silk may actually be explosive.

FAST LIFE, SHORT LIFE: THE WAGES OF SIN

Though Victoria, and BC, were many weeks travel from Europe in the 19th century, Europe still held sway over many an imagination, and weeks-old newspapers were eagerly read by the city's literate class. This isn't a BC story, but Victoria residents could nonetheless read it with their morning coffee. Well, maybe not with their coffee: after this sad tale, dear reader might think twice, and head for the tea caddy. This account of death caused by dissolute living combines prurience and judgment. Who knew coffee and women were equally ruinous? The Victoria *Daily British Colonist* told the story on January 4, 1867:

> Call the roll of the young men of 1830, says a Paris paper, and ask where are they? De Balzac is dead—coffee killed him. Frederick Soulie is dead—the victim of coffee and licentiousness. Eugene Briffant died a madman... Grandville went mad, and breathed his last in a private insane asylum. Lasalle died... a raving lunatic. Love Weimers died from opium eating and licentiousness. Rabbe, after suffering agony from a loathsome disease, took poison to end his prolonged torture. Alfred Musset died a victim to the bottle and the cigar. Count Alfred d'Orsay was killed by cigars and licentiousness. Henry Beyley from coffee and women. Hyppolyte Royer Collard died from coffee and tobacco, Gerard de Nerval, after oscillation between plenty and want, abstemiousness and licentiousness, went mad and hung himself... Eugene Sue's name is added to the fatal list—coffee and women were his ruin.

FAT MEN

From the Zeballos *Miner*, March 21, 1938:

> It is understood that, while the government intends to construct a float for planes and small boats at the wharf, which is fast nearing completion, only a ladder is provided from the float up to the wharf. This is going to be

decidedly inconvenient for women and children, and the occasional fat man.

FIREARMS AND FOLLY

Somehow, in Western movies, guns always fire properly and accidents never occur. Truth is, 19th-century guns were less than reliable, and the average gun-toter not much better. Sometimes, the combination of the two was more than unfortunate; stories abound of men shot by mistake. There were rarely any serious penalties for such carelessness. And could it be coincidence that both victims of these 1859 shootings were black men in a time when blacks were greatly outnumbered by white Americans? From the Victoria *Daily British Colonist* on July 22, 1859:

> On the afternoon of the 2nd, a colored man named Washington Sims, who was working a claim opposite the mouth of the Bridge River, had occasion to cross in a canoe to a store, and agreed to ferry two Frenchmen over. When about mid-way in the stream, one of the latter who had brought a gun with him, rose to change his position and in so doing the weapon exploded, literally blowing out the heart of Sims, who was steering. Sims was from San Francisco, was aged about 35 years, and was noted for his Herculean frame, being over six feet two inches in height, and stout in proportion. The Frenchman was severely censured for his carelessness.
>
> On Fourth of July morning, an estimable young colored man, named Thomas Lewis, was killed at Follows store on Boston Bar, by a Cornish miner, who was in the habit of cocking a pistol the hammer of which slipped from his thumb. Lewis was shot through the left breast and

died instantly. An inquest was held on the body by the miners, and a verdict fully exonerating the Cornishman was returned.

FISH STOREYS

Newcomers to the district always provided amusement—though sometimes the stories became a little heavy-handed. And the spin given to the story depended very much on the editor-reporter. One editor reported with a straight face the plans of a new settler in the Bulkley Valley in the first decade of the 20th century, but left it to the reader to judge who was the joker, who the jokee. From the Aldermere *Bulkley Pioneer* on April 10, 1908:

> A new departure in the way of amusement is being inaugurated by one of our worthy sons of Britain. Since the desirable land is mostly taken up and the late amendment to the land act allows for the disposal of foreshore and land under rivers and lakes he has taken possession of a lonely island in the Skeena opposite Kitselas, where he will engage in piscatorial research and study. To provide against contingencies a wonderful structure of cedar logs five stories high with a window, door and landing place on each story will be built. When the June freshets come on and a subaqueous [effect] prevails upon the rawnch, and the silver-sided sockeye together with the formidable hump-back salmon are entertaining their friends upon the succulent roots and animalculea of the ground floor an ascent is made to the next floor, while the murky torrent outside fleets by the only window gurgling to a sympathetic gurgle going on within. He may be aroused

from sleep by the clammy snout of a sockeye jabbing him in the ribs; then the upward movement is repeated, and perhaps in the end the buoyant and self contained master of this submarine ranch will find himself afloat upon turbulent waters. Then he will have a lookout for the line of least resistance by the largest whirlpools to the mainland, which should provide a novel and interesting diversion.

FLIM-FLAM MAN

Everyone knows about and some succumb to the flim-flam man from Nigeria who invades your e-mail with a wondrous opportunity to make money: help him get his money out of the country by sending a much smaller amount, a paltry $10,000 or maybe $50,000, overseas, to release the larger amount, and you will be rich—and help a fellow man into the bargain. But the origins of this flim-flam trick date much further back than e-mail, though the fleecing must have been considerably slower and more laborious. The Spanish Prisoner con game, for example, was first recorded in 1588, when a girl approached various British nobleman, requesting help in ransoming her father, also supposedly of the British nobility, from a Spanish prison.

This Spanish Prisoner scam was remarkably long-lived, reaching BC in the 20th century. "Older than the everlasting hills and apparently as useful as ever" was the way that the Victoria *Daily Colonist* characterized the "Spanish flim-flam" in 1909.[2] Someone who claimed to be immured in a Spanish prison wrote to a Victoria man declaring that hidden baggage checks would lead to a suitcase containing more than a million francs. The prisoner needed just a fraction of this amount to pay the creditors, secure his release and reclaim his fortune. Then the Victoria recipient would be paid one-third of the total. But the money from Victoria must not, on any account, be sent to the prison, since all mail sent prisonwards was automatically opened. Instead, it must be sent to the prisoner's "servant," who would do the necessary.

"Burton resident offered fortune," read the headline in the Nakusp *Silver Standard* on June 14, 1934, a front-page excitement that the paper promptly debunked. "Burton is on the Spanish prisoner [fraud]," reported the paper, "Robert Faulds, well-known Burton rancher, having just received the first 'come-on' letter from the mythical inmate of a Spanish prison with secret wealth to share." The letter was identical to one received by a Nelson man the week before.

It offered the recipient $120,000, a sizeable fortune in those Depression days, if he would simply forward the money necessary to defend "S," a prisoner in a Spanish jail. Once released, S would retrieve money held in a secret pocket in a hidden portmanteau. The scam, the newspaper suggested, was generations old; two years before, another man had received a similar appeal to help a prisoner in a Mexican jail.

None of those who reported the flim-flam to the police or the papers sent the money. But, if the success of the present-day Nigerian scam is anything to go by, anxious eyes in a variety of BC towns must have scanned the mail each morning, eagerly awaiting their windfall.

FLOURY SOLUTIONS

In steamboat days, a boat ran into a rock on the Skeena River and was holed. The captain grounded the ship on a river bar. Paul, a Japanese crew member, dived in to take a look at the hole. When he surfaced, he asked the captain for a sack of flour, surreptitiously whisked away from the purser who was vigilant in keeping track of supplies. Paul cut some wood, plugged the hole with the sack of flour and nailed planks and braces over it. The crew siphoned out the water that had leaked in, and the boat was refloated, to continue its journey up the Skeena and back, at which point she was repaired in a more traditional fashion as the purser continued to puzzle over his missing sack of flour.[3]

FLYING AND FALLING

The first hot-air balloon flight took place in 1783, but it was in the latter half of the 19th century, particularly in the 1890s, that such flights attracted huge crowds to exhibitions and fairs across western Canada. Often, though, weather conditions or problems with the huge balloons prevented the ascents. And sometimes balloonists would have been better off had they aborted their flights. In New Westminster in 1894, the spectators' "oohs" and "ahs" turned to screams of dismay and distress, as the manned balloon plummeted to the earth, with the inevitable death of its pilot.

Professor Sopher, described as a Puget Sound balloonist, brought his flying balloon to the mainland city in mid-October. For some reason, Sopher decided not to go aloft, took the $300 the New Westminster fair authorities paid him for his ascent, and hired for a small sum a neophyte, Charles Marble, to make three flights. Marble, according to reports, strutted about in his pink tights, getting the balloon ready for the first flight. "The immense canvas monster of the air was put in position, a few holes sewn up, and a wood and coal fire built underneath, so that smoke, gas and all entered the balloon, and slowly, very slowly, the great bulk swelled ... About 4 o'clock the great monster was full." Some

8,000 people gathered to watch, "the guys were loosened and the balloon ascended, swift as a rocket. First the great bulk, the yards of rope, then the folded parachute, then more yards of rope, then a trapeze, and dangling in the air at the end of it all was the figure of Marble."

The crowd thought Marble would drop with the parachute. He did not. The balloon began to descend. The parachute did not drop. The balloon disappeared from spectators' view, straight into the river. Boats hurried to Marble's aid; he was found, insensible, tied into the trapeze. Rushed to a nearby hotel, he died not long after. "He was taken . . . to a warm room, a mistake so often made in case of threatened death by drowning," sermonized the paper, "for the patient should always be attended in the open air."

Sopher seemed unfazed. He hired another daredevil for the next flight. But customs officers seized the balloon, demanding a fee if it were to ascend once more. As they argued, darkness fell and ascent was impossible.

Marble had desperately needed the $10 he would have received for the flight, the Victoria *Daily Colonist* reported. The autopsy showed he died of a heart stoppage, probably, it was said, literally frightened to death.[4]

Though many New Westminster residents saw the tragic event, the *Daily Columbian* all but ignored it, leaving it to the Victoria newspaper to tell the story. Instead, the *Columbian* filled column after column with exhibition news and civic boosterism, reporting on prizes for poultry from barred Plymouth Rocks to Black Spanish hens, the magnificent fruits and vegetables on display and the prospects for the district, relegating the accident to a small squib on the inquest, where no blame was attached but mentioning that the men who rushed their boats to the drowning man were to be paid for their services, and a paragraph about sending Marble's body home to Washington State.

FLU, 1919

The influenza pandemic of 1918–19 killed some 4,000 people in BC, more than one quarter of them native people, a number vastly out of proportion to their total numbers. This account of several deaths, though sympathetic, contains a chilling reference to "good Indians," perhaps an allusion to the 19th-century aphorism that the only good Indian was a dead Indian. From the Prince George *Citizen*, February 5, 1919:

> Chila is dead. To the great world this means nothing, but the Peace River voyageur will remember with a passing regret the story of the lone teepee on the hillside by the Hudson's Bay Company post, where for the past seventeen years the crippled Indian lay, an example of cheerful adversity to the rest of the world. Attacked by rheumatism seventeen years ago, following exposure on a hunting trip, this once famous hunter has had since that time for his world a little path of about fifty yards over which he propelled himself with his elbows to a small garden, which he cultivated while lying on his back.

The recent flu epidemic also claimed for a victim Montagneuse, the big chief of the Beaver Indians. Several sub-chiefs and several of the best hunters of the tribe have also gone to swell the ranks of the good Indians. The passing of Montagneuse marks practically the end of a regime faithful to the traditions of the Hudson's Bay Company in this region.

FUN AND GAMES

Every pioneer town had its amusements, with sports days, carnivals, contests and competitions. Some were more amusing than others. From the Bella Coola *Courier* on May 31, 1913:

The attention of all is now directed towards the games and sports of the afternoon, which take on a hilariously amusing character. Among the funniest of these are the sack race, in which Mr. F. Grant acquits himself with amazing agility; the egg and spoon race of the ladies; the bolster-bar contest, in which the opponents, facing each other, sit astride a slippery round-sided bar, and buffet one another with canvas bags stuffed with hay, trying to unseat the vis-à-vis with dexterous pommelling; the tug-of-war, contested by Indians and whites, in which the battle was won by the Indians, among whom were several exceedingly large, fat and hefty specimens; the greased pole, the ham at the top of which was won by a dark horse, a little boy who slipped suddenly into the competition, announced that he was going to win, and did so with apparent absence of effort.

Five mile, half mile and one mile races were run. The winner of the five mile marathon was Jim Kelly, an Indian, an athlete of great speed and endurance. He had to fight hard for his laurels, however, against Mr. Theodore Levelton, who won the championship cup last year, and may, next . . . The Indians simply simmer, boil over and froth with glee, mixed with a touch of sly jocose malice at their victories over their white brethren: in their cyclonic winner, Jim Kelly, who sweeps everything before him, earning many prizes; and in their tug-of-war, Waterloo to the whites.

GAMBLERS

Whisky, women and song were supposedly the mainstay of a lonely bachelor's life in the outback—but gambling was right up there with them. Down at the end of Main Street in every boom town, card players gathered in a backroom to battle each other or to be fleeced by the con men and card sharps from out of town. Despite frequent editorial campaigns to have the gamblers run out of town, somehow they stayed. The police often turned a blind eye to the gambling, usually counting on a payoff under the table.

Sandon, the bustling mining town in the West Kootenay, was

sometimes known as the Monte Carlo of Canada, where miners could get rid of their wages or pokes playing poker or blackjack, roulette, faro or craps. Fire destroyed most of Sandon in May of 1900, but it didn't take the gamblers long to set up right in the middle of the street, or so the story goes. But no boom town lasts forever, and, as the silver rush subsided, the professional gamblers departed, looking for other suckers in other boom towns. Wrote Robert Lowery, newspaper editor, "It's all off now. Chips that pass in the night are valuable only for souvenirs . . . The dealers, boosters, chair-warmers, pluggers, crappers, professional rubber-neckers, markers, rimmers, crimpers, short card men, Montana sleeve artists and other members of the sporting fraternity will have to turn their backs on the classic shades of the Silver City."[5]

Even the tiny fishing and cannery town of Port Essington attracted professional gamblers and saw many working men out to prove they could beat the tables or the cards. In 1907, a police constable took a room in the hotel and spent some time there with a waitress. When she was fired, he demanded that she be reinstated or he would close down the hotel's card room.

The hotel said, "Close it and be damned." The constable rushed to the blackjack table, gave the dealer ten minutes to close it all down, and left the hotel "amid a volley of the most obscene language the writer has ever heard." The constable came back at midnight, tried to brawl with the editor of the *Sun*, then left again, defeated.

The editor, who seems to have been a gambler himself, described the gambling scene: "The clink of silver dollars can be heard by children and passers by at every hour of the day or night." The two men in charge, who leased the premises from another police constable, declared they paid no "direct" licence fee to run their four poker tables and a chuck-a-luck layout—a table dice game that was the origin of the phrase "tinhorn gambler," after the tin chute that the dice rattled down.

Down the street, the newspaperman found a backroom gambling den behind the cigar store. This room had fifty men of all nationalities crowded around three blackjack tables and a chuck-a-luck layout.

"Space will not permit us to treat this subject in the manner we would have liked," concluded the editor, piously and hypocritically, but readers could rest assured that he would comment again on the gambling in Port Essington, as well as on the rottenness in official quarters.[6]

GETTING THE GOATS

Some stories leave the reader hanging: the Bella Coola *Courier* did not report on whether the Hendricks got the goats, and if they did, how they were transported to the man who requested them. Dr. French was in charge of a natural history museum in Washington, and had a permit allowing him to export the goats. From the *Courier*, November 9, 1912:

> The Hendricks brothers have left town for a hunt at the head of South Bentinck Arm. Their reports of this occasion will undoubtedly embrace some novel features, as

they are going to try to fill an order for eight live mountain goats. Their return to Bella Coola is expected to rival the annual visit of Santa Claus and his reindeer. When last seen Charlie and Jesse had not decided whether to lead, drive or ride the goats, but in any case we wish them joy.

The goats are required by Dr. Cecil French, of Washington D.C., who also required two adult mountain sheep and a specimen of the inland white bear, to be found on Gribble and Princess Royal Islands. The price offered is $150 a head alive.

GETTING TO KNOW YOU
From the Phoenix *Pioneer*, April 1, 1911:

Nearly everyone knows Charley Flood. There are four drummers who did not know Charley, but now they are well acquainted with him.

A few days ago Charley went into a cafe in Rossland to get a lunch. While waiting on his repast he fell asleep. Four drummers whose spirits had come in contact with some other spirits thought to have some fun with the sleeping guest.

While one of them kicked him on the shins, the others poured salt into his hair and otherwise amused themselves at his expense. Finally Charley woke up. He surveyed the situation carefully and then started to clean up the knights of the grip.

Now these gentlemen had never heard of Charley. They were not aware that he could lick his weight in wild cats about four times, but they are wiser now.

Among the four was a big bruiser to whom Charley directed his attention first. He was compelled to land on him twice before he succumbed to the terrific onslaught. The others fared the same fate, and they all lay on the floor in silence fearful that the dose might be repeated.

After the fracas the travelling men held a conference and agreed that their newly formed acquaintance was the "white man's hope," and will prevail upon Mr. Flood to immediately go into training to meet the colored champion of the fistic arena.

GHOSTS

There's many a ghostly tale told in every town in BC, as windows rattle, maidens weep, and phantoms you can pass your arm right through appear at the top of the stairs at midnight. Almost every good ghost story includes lost love, or lost treasure, or lost homes, or murder most foul. And not a few include dogs that bay at nothing humans can see—though very few include cats, who are much too sensible to worry about anything or anyone incapable of providing food. Sometimes, the ghost walks among wary and suspicious men. Reported the Victoria *Daily Colonist* on November 8, 1898:

> Mrs. McDonald, housekeeper for Engineer Hoare of the steamer Aberdeen, says Mr. Hoare refuses to live in his house on the swamp road because a tramp he had given a glass of water to last year, and whose dead body was found shortly after in the mountains, has appeared to him in the identical spot on the anniversary of his first appearance. He waked up the house and the tramp sank from view in the swamp. A strange dog has been lying

near the spot since. Several other residents claim to have seen the alleged ghost.

The *Daily Colonist* told another story on November 24, 1903:

There is a ghost walking at Ladysmith who will meet a large-sized bunch of trouble if any of the men folk of the nearby port lay hands upon him. He has been walking for three weeks at Ladysmith and has caused no small amount of fright to some of the more timid residents, one young boy named Kerr being sick as the result of the fright received and a woman was given quite a shock as a result of seeing the white-clad spook.

The "ghost" is believed to be a colored man, at least some of those who have seen him when he has been putting his ghostly garb over his head and shoulders say he is. The police have been searching for him, and if found it will likely go hard with him.

His last appearance was to Mr. McNicholl, a Ladysmith tailor. He sprang out from behind some bushes one night last week as the tailor was going home. "Come and have a drink," said the ghost.

"You'd better move on," said the knight of the needle, "or I'll put a shot through you."

"All right," said the accommodating ghost, who was wearing a sheet and the customary ghostly paraphernalia, "if that's the way you feel about it, I'll move on."

Night after night, the ghost, wearing his sheet and a white shining mask, goes on the war path and frightens many. When two young people were taking a short cut to a dance, he sprang out upon them, and they ran for the hall to get assistance. When they returned, the "ghost" had vanished.

Some of the younger citizens have been dressing as women in the hope that the "ghost" will attempt to frighten them, so that they can capture him, but he failed to appear for them.

The ghost scare is the talk of the port and the captain of a steamer which was loading coal there some days ago was telling of how little fright he would have if he saw the ghost.

One of the engineers secured a sheet, and when the captain was coming to the wharf after dark, he sprang out and frightened the skipper badly. The captain made for the gangplank at a two-minute clip.

GOLD FISH

Fish stories usually involve the one that got away, but one Okanagan resident caught not only his fish, but also something of greater value, though not as palatable. The Nelson *News* told the tale in 1908:

Friend the other day sent Mr. Simms, manager of the Hudson's Bay store, a "squawfish," caught in the Okanagan Lake, says the Okanagan. It was a big one, and although these fish do not make toothsome eating for most people, Mr. Simms has acquired a keen relish for them. He took the fish home and had it prepared for dinner and here is where the interesting part comes in; for on opening the fish, in the maw was found a small nickel bound lady's pocketbook. With much excitement the purse was opened and found to contain a ten dollar gold piece and a C.P.R. ticket. Mr. Simms is naturally delighted with his luck and places a big value on his tenner. These fish, it is said, will swallow almost anything that comes their way.

He has often found all manner of things in them. It is supposed that a lady travelling on the lake steamer lost her purse overboard. A few weeks ago someone was advertising a lost purse of such description. She was a stranger and unfortunately her name was not taken. If this should meet her eye Mr. Simms would be pleased to give her ten dollars but not the gold piece. He proposes to hold onto that.

GRAVE TALES

From the Atlin *Claim*, November 25, 1899:

On the door of a neat cabin on Lake street may be seen the following: "For rent. Apply personally to Paddy O'Brien, Kilarney Avenue, Dublin, Ireland. Private graveyard on the premises for use, (free of charge) for tenants who fail to pay the rent, or are found frozen to death."

GROUNDHOG DAY

Tradition has it that, if the groundhog sees his shadow on February 2, we're in for six more weeks of winter. Tradition in BC has it that (a) there are no groundhogs in the province, (b) anywhere outside of the southwest corner, we're in for at least six more weeks of winter regardless of sun or cloud and (c) if it's a good story, why not run with it? That's what the Portland Canal *News* did, moving on to a fantasy about the groundhog's alter ego on February 4, 1927:

> About 11 o'clock the clouds broke and some blue sky, enough to patch a pair of overalls appeared.
>
> But lo, and behold, up the canal came a pall of stygian darkness, and again the feathers flew.
>
> However, at 1 o'clock, or maybe 1:10, Old Sol broke through long enough to cast shadows all over the landscape as well as on the hopes of the community.
>
> Of course, in this country we have no real groundhogs, their cousins, the whistlers [marmots], holding their proxies... whistling for dogs and then dodging into his den. If cornered, he bites long strips of hide out of the dog's face, and caches it for trophies to show his children.
>
> Perhaps the whistler will not have as much effect on spring as the genuine groundhog, but he is mean enough to, at that.

GROUSING

Too many cooks spoil the broth, or, in this case, the grouse in an anecdote from *BC 1887, A Ramble in British Columbia*:

> We sat round the fire, six in number, and one commenced operations by plucking the grouse and sticking it on a long skewer which was fixed in the ground so that it leant a little over the fire. Thus it was roasted for about half an hour, when somebody woke up and said, "I think I should put a scrap of onion in it." So another took four or five onions and crammed them with difficulty into the interior of the bird. Then the roasting proceeded for a space, and another said, "I should turn it like this," whereupon he turned it upside down, and the onions rolled out upon the carpet grass that is and were placed upon the fire, and their perfume was grateful. Then another searcher after truth said solemnly, "I think and I have not scamped the thinking that it ought to be split." And it was split, and again the roasting went on. Finally an impatient one said, "Let's finish that d___d rooster in the morning," and it was placed outside the lodge to cool. While there a wanderer trod upon it and rolled it in the sand, which abounded in that place; and in the morning being frozen harder than a rock, it was divided with difficulty and a hatchet, and fried; and with one voice the people cried out "Delicious."

Chapter Four

Hangmen, Highwaymen, Horses and Hens

HALLOWE'EN HIJINKS

From the Queen Charlotte *Islander*, November 6, 1911:

> There was the sound of "revelry by night" at Beattie's on Hallowe'en, "George" being the host of a gay surprise party. Chief engineer Wilson of the Prince Albert sang, the talking machine played and everybody was happy. There was a hat-trimming competition for the men, in which Mr. Beattie won the prize, a Japanese umbrella, and a pencil-sharpening competition for the ladies. Refreshments and a little dancing closed a pleasant evening.

HANGMEN

As long as there were hangings, there was a need for an official hangman. And why not apply for the job if you thought your qualifications were appropriate? Civil service pay, steady work, maybe even job satisfaction? In 1895, a man by the name of James Dupen applied for the job. "I executed Albert Stroeble at Victoria on the 30th of January 1894 while I was at Victoria in the name of W.B. Jones and done my duty well as Mr. Miller the Sheriff and Chief Warden Johns can tell you and as I see there has been 2 Executions since and likely to be more I would like to offer my services as Public Executioner for BC at a reasonable figer or sum I have been in the English Navy for 23 years and I receive a pension from it, with 23 years very good references."[1] Dupen didn't get the job; he next appears advertising as a cleaner of clothes in Victoria in 1902.

A letter to the attorney general in 1894 reminded the sheriff of New Westminster that the writer, J.R. Radcliffe, had been appointed as the Dominion hangman, and that New Westminster needed only to pay his expenses if they wanted him to execute one Hugh Lynn. To that point, Radcliffe had been best known for inventing a supposedly better method of hanging. Unfortunately, when he tested his new method, the condemned man took many minutes to die, so he returned to the more conventional method.

Eight years later, Radcliffe was reported to have broken down after an execution and wept like a child, declaring to the press that he did not like his job, but he could get no other. Shortly thereafter, he was in Kamloops for an execution; he was back in 1905 and 1906. On these occasions, there was no report of tears, though on his way east in 1906, he fell against a car door and was expected to lose the sight of one eye; later reports suggested he drank to excess. On one other occasion, he was perturbed since he was not sure the man he was about to hang was guilty, and was greatly relieved when the prisoner confessed.

On December 18, 1908, Radcliffe executed three men simultaneously at New Westminster. The *Daily Colonist* reported the following day:

> With a sarcastic smile on his face, Pertella, the negro who murdered Mrs. Jenkins, looked direct at the husband of his victim and dropped into eternity at ten minutes past eight this morning. Next to him stood Jenkins, murderer of Mrs. Morrison at Hazelmere, and shoulder to shoulder with him stood Lee Chung, who killed Yong Ah Hing. The proceedings were mercifully short, and the three were executed simultaneously.
>
> It was the first triple hanging in the Dominion of Canada, and never did three criminals meet death in a more impassive way. All ate hearty meals last night, and Pertella had to be called twice from his sleep this morning

to partake of breakfast. The scaffold was built in the courtyard of the Jail, and about a hundred persons were present at the execution. The three murderers were brought on to the scaffold just after 8 o'clock, Pertella and Lee Chung being handcuffed and Jenkins having his arms strapped behind his back. They were absolutely impassive, although as Radcliffe, the executioner, adjusted the black caps the Chinaman began to quiver and Jenkins showed the faintest trace of emotion. Pertella gazed down into the face of the husband of his victim and smiled.

Staff captain Collier, of the Salvation Army, asked Jenkins who was the only one who had not confessed, whether he had anything to say, but received no answer and withdrew to the edge of the scaffold reciting the Lord's Prayer: "Forgive us our trespasses," he said.

"Stand clear, gentlemen," remarked Radcliffe, and pulled the lever and the three disappeared from view.

Pertella was apparently killed instantaneously, Jenkins quivered for a moment after the drop and Lee Chung's hands opened and shut once.

Then the Jury was sworn in, a formal Inquest held and the jury coming out from the jail met the undertakers carrying in three plain coffins. The execution was over.

The execution may well have been the first simultaneous triple hanging in Canada, but British Columbia had an earlier quadruple hanging, when the McLean boys and Alex Hare were put to death in 1881 for the murder of a police constable and a shepherd. Radcliffe continued to work as Canada's executioner until he died in 1912, at the age of 55, from excessive drinking. Records are extremely vague, but he hanged between 69 and 150 people.

HENS, PILFERED

The comings and goings of chickens were always good for a newspaper story or two. One such account appeared in the police court news of the Victoria *Daily British Colonist* on January 1, 1878:

> Quin Que, a Chinaman charged with having unlawfully in his possession a hen the property of Pilot Revely, valued at 75 cents and upwards.
>
> ... Pilot Revely said that on Sunday morning between 9 and 10 o'clock he found the prisoner in possession of the hen produced, on Cormorant street; the said hen was stolen from his premises on the Saturday night; had lost four hens besides this one.
>
> Chong Lee said the prisoner bought the chicken from him on Sunday morning.
>
> His Honor discharged Quin Que; but said he considered that the case should be enquired into as he certainly did not think the hen produced was a Chinese hen. He would if necessary issue a summons for the original owner of the hen to appear.

HENS' TEETH

From the Ashcroft *Journal*, January 8, 1916:

> At Christmas a lady in Ashcroft, while cleaning a chicken for the pot, found in the gizzard a human, gold-filled tooth. This had evidently been picked up by the rooster

for a piece of gravel. Owner can have same by proving property.

HERMITS

Many a lost or purposefully lonely soul has taken up residence on an island shore or in a mountain valley. But the desire to be left alone means that the death of a hermit is rarely noted. Not so the hermit of Trial Island. In 1894, a Victoria *Daily Colonist* squib declared, "The body of the Trial Island hermit will likely be exhumed this week by gold seekers. Before the unfortunate man started out on the expedition that terminated in his drowning, he borrowed $50 in gold from a friend, and the supposition is that when his body was found the gold in his pocket was overlooked, as owing to the decomposed state of the body it was interred as quickly as possible. Now there is some talk of digging up the body to recover the gold if possible."

The *Daily Colonist* never says whether the body was, in fact, disinterred. The newspaper had been more interested when hermit John Kergan was alive, discovering him when a reporter hitched a ride with a provincial police boat that fetched up at Trial Island, where Kergan had built a cabin. The policeman declared that a booby trap that would explode a cartridge if anyone opened his door must be dismantled. Meanwhile, the reporter admired sketches the hermit had made and marvelled at salt distilled from seawater, blocks of compressed jam made from island berries, rolled fruit sheets made by a process Kergan had invented, smoked clams, a small windmill that ran a saw (also home made) and a forge.

What do you do on Sunday, the reporter inquired. "Well, I sit down and have a church of my own. I can think as I like then."[2]

The reporter showed so much respect for the abilities and intelligence of the hermit that others crossed the waves to visit him. So many others, in fact, that Kergan fled from this forced conviviality to yet another small island. The trip to Victoria for supplies was a difficult one, and in May of 1894, he was lost at sea. His boat was found first, his body some days later.

Someone who knew and admired him wrote, "This man with a single round saw, which he worked either by wind or water power, would cut up cedar planks from drift wood, and with hammer and nails construct a water tight boat . . ." The writer praised Kergan's artistic ability and his great inventiveness, which reached to making plans for an air engine to drive his boat. "His sterling qualities of uprightness, honesty and straightforwardness were made known to all who came across him . . . The writer has reason to suppose that John Kergan, the hermit of Trial Island, was pure in soul and manly in character, as well as gifted above the average of his fellow-man, whose company he so strangely shunned."[3]

HIGHWAYMEN

The stagecoach is rollicking along the trail, the horses in fine fettle, the driver erect on the box, the passengers inside snoozing or schmoozing. The coach slows for a corner and out of the bushes springs the highwayman, aiming his rifle and demanding, "Your money or your life."

The driver puts up heroic resistance and is shot for his pains. The damsels weep, the gentlemen give in to the inevitable, and the highwayman rides off with his spoils. At least, that's the way the story is supposed to go. In BC, of course, nothing went according to stereotype.

Take, for example, the stagecoach holdup that occurred place in Atlin in 1899. The stage left town one Monday evening. The stagecoach driver took a nap while someone else handled the reins. According to the newspaper account, driver Walker's dreams were sweet: "From time to time a smile flitted across his countenance, as he murmured, 'I'm fat' or 'Pay me.'" The stage started up the big hill leading out of town, and then it stopped, and the command "Throw up your hands" rudely awakened Walker. There stood a masked man with a Winchester repeating rifle. "Quick as thought up went Walker's hands—a plug of blackstrap in one and a corncob pipe in the other. Meanwhile the other occupants littered the bottom of the stage with their mining licences and other valuables." A passenger named Patterson suddenly recalled he had $300 plus some gold nuggets with him; not wanting to give them up, he dropped from the coach and ran back down the hill. "Corrected time gives his speed as 3 min. 40 secs, he only having touched the high spots." Good idea, thought some of the other passengers, and they too took to the woods.

The others obeyed the highwayman. "Photographer Draper said he would donate a dozen photographs done in the most approved style in lieu of cash. This was indignantly refused by the bl-u-u-dy villain, who remarked this was strictly a cash transaction and offers of placer claims, hydraulic leases and other articles of doubtful value would not be considered. Then a choice selection of poker chips, jackknives, plugged quarters, etc., was deposited on the ground. An inventory showed the highwayman had realized $4.70 and the contempt of his victims from his daring deed. Having pocketed the swag, he backed into the bushes, remarking he must have struck a crowd of newspaper people."

Meanwhile, the escapees were soon out of sight. "An old lady," the newspaper reported, "... who is said to have defective hearing, also took French leave and followed closely on Patterson for a couple of hundred yards. But Patterson finding her locomotion too uncertain down the hill and too gallant, of course, to desert, he offered to make himself a vehicle for the while. 'No,' she said, 'I'm be blowed if I do; I'd rather chance going back and handing over my two Willow creek nuggets than face a 45-angled hill on the back of any man.'"

Back in town, news of the holdup reached the police chief, who had apparently just finished reading a tale of terror and retribution in the Yukon. He summoned up half a dozen men, and off they went, searching high and low, and capturing, or so the newspaper said, a pair of pants that might have belonged to the highwayman. Why they were absent from their owner, the newspaper did not say. But of the highwayman himself, nothing could be found.

All's well that ends well, might have been the refrain. But the highwayman himself was not happy with the accounts. Some time later, he wrote to friends in Pine City, near Atlin, from his "hideout" a few miles up the line at Bennett. He had been sadly misled, he complained. "They weren't the people I expected. I could hardly keep from laughing when Maude Biggs, poor girl, made an attempt to dig up. She asked me if I wanted a black-jack. She was game though and shook less than the other members of the party." And, wrote the man, he was pretty sure the police chief knew who was responsible, because he appeared everywhere the highwayman went—causing him to leave town, though by boat, not on the next stage. The newspaper's comment: "This fellow appears to be as cool as a cucumber, but he better not try that game too often on this side of the line."

And that, it appears, was the end of that. Though not, of course, of highwaymen in BC, who continued to rob stagecoaches, as they had since the 1860s. The 1890s were a particularly busy time for such bandits. In 1890, for example, a lone highwayman wearing a mask made from a piece of flour sack robbed the Cariboo stage of more than $4,000 in gold nuggets and dust. The driver challenged him, saying he could not frighten them with an old umbrella, but rethought his challenge when the highwayman, hiding in a bush, said he had a rifle and a shotgun trained on the driver. Many were suspected but none were caught in this robbery.

In 1894, a highwayman held up the stage when it was a half hour out of 150 Mile House. The description of said highwayman was remarkably detailed, coming from the driver and the passenger who shared the outside seat and who were, after all, not that close to the miscreant. But then, who are we to quibble? "He was a tall man," they reported, "of five feet nine or ten, very quick and agile. His gray eyes were sharp and keen, seen through two holes in a hastily constructed mask made from a piece of gunny sack which completely covered his face and hair. The hands that held the rifle quivered as though the highwayman were very nervous, though his voice was calm." The report continued, "The police have a good clue to the desperado's identity, as his gunnysack mask has been identified by the settler from whose house the material was taken by a stranger who passed the night there."

The police were perhaps not always so logical. At Eagle Pass in 1885, during the construction of the railway, two men arrested on suspicion of being the highwaymen who had committed several holdups were released. "The real highwayman, who wore a mask," reported the paper, "and is an old man, has got away. He was a harmless highwayman, for those who would not stop at his command were not fired at."[4]

HOCKEY, SORT OF

Sandon *Paystreak* editor Robert Lowery could introduce humour even into his account of a hockey game. He wrote on February 25, 1899:

> On Thursday evening at 8.30 in the Sandon rink, one of the most remarkable interpretations of hockey yet perpetrated on an unsuspecting public was sprung on the innocents of Sandon . . .

> The puck was faced off at 8.30 and one-fifth of a second later all hands were in the middle of a scrimmage. The scrimmage lasted until the end of the game. Kaslo played

a rocky game, but for the first while Sandon played worse. Inside of ten minutes, the puck wandered into the Sandon goal and Kaslo cheered. Three minutes later Sandon made a goal and everyone cheered. From that out the play was fast and furious. Each team played indiscriminately for the other end of the rink. Rules are at a discount and combinations considered superfluous. McVichie fell down 47 times inside of 15 minutes, and never lit twice in the same place. Andy Grierson saw the puck three times that he remembers of. Conneley and Frosty, the Kaslo champions, played shinney like they used to in Cobokonk. Jack Crawford left Sam Hunter piled up in a hole in the wall and Bert Dill got so well posted that his bumps would lead a phrenologist to believe that his wife used a rolling pin to enhance connubial felicity. Oh! It was a warm game.

At the end of the first half the mud flaters [Kasloites] were astonished to find they had five goals while the cliff-dwellers [Sandonians] had only three.

During the ten minute pause the smoke cleared away and off they were again. This time it was for gore. McVichie continued his tactics, playing on his hands and knees. Bob Hammond shot a goal from somewhere near the other end, Birchall played forward while Hood took his place in goal and made some grand stand runs. The Sandon boys crowded the Kasloites into corners and dark alleys and made another goal, which evened the score. At the call of time it stood at 5 to 5, and both sides seemed satisfied to quit.

A sort of aftermath will be arranged to take place in Kaslo at an early date under the auspices of the Victorian Order of Nurses.

> A reward of $10,000 will be offered by the Humane Society for the apprehension and conviction of the parties who told McVichie that he knew something about hockey.
>
> As a matter of charity, the names of the players are suppressed.

HOMELESS

The homeless are not a modern phenomenon. The Phoenix *Pioneer* complained on January 21, 1911:

> Vags and hoboes are becoming too numerous in Phoenix. The police should clear the city of these shiftless characters as they are only trouble brewers. No person without evident means of earning his bread should be tolerated within the city limits.

HORSE LAUGH

From the Rossland *Miner*, September 6, 1899:

> A most laughable feature of the day was afforded by an advertising fake prepared by Fry, the grocer. Charley Burton was induced to make up as a Palouse [Palouse refers to a farming region in the northwestern U.S.] farmer, and drive along Columbia avenue in a farm cart loaded with live poultry, cabbages, pumpkins and other produce. All went well until the horse attached to the cart saw the painters' union; then all went wrong with Burton. The horse wheeled around and dashed towards the rocky bluff, scattering cabbages, chickens, hay and

pumpkins along the street, and scattering the crowd in every direction. The unfortunate driver, who was a novice at the farmer business, clung desperately to the reins, and after an unsuccessful attempt to drive up Red mountain, managed to stop the horse on the edge of a steep bank of West Columbia avenue. The incident afforded unbounded amusement to the large crowd which had gathered in anticipation of the horse races.

HORSE NEWS

Frightened horses, wayward horses and plain ornery horses created problems just as automobiles would in later years—though with considerably less carnage. On May 2, 1911, in Prince Rupert, the *Daily News* sternly lectured horsemen after an "affrighted team" of horses galloped along the main plank street and fell on a turn, with one horse killed but no women or children injured:

> There is a regulation in the Streets Traffic By-law passed by the late city council to the effect that every horse left standing on the street must have a sixteen pound weight attached to the bridle. It is safe to say that few in Prince Rupert have seen a horse tethered to a weight on our streets. No attempt has been made to enforce the regulation. Indeed, the Mayor when asked about the matter this morning did not know there was such a regulation in the city by-laws.
>
> Whatever necessity there may be to enforce such a by-law in other cities, the need is doubled in Prince Rupert. With no wide streets for leeway, or pavements to take refuge on, our women and children are at the mercy

of runaway teams. Even to the strong man, who may attempt the task of stopping them, the personal hazard is increased by the narrowness of the plankways.

HORSES, NO GOOD

From the Aldermere *Bulkley Pioneer*, August 17, 1907:

Some horsemen visited Moricetown last week and sold Mooskin Jimmy three steeds which he claimed are "no good"—one outlaw and two skates. Jimmy and some of his neighbors argued the point with the traders with the result that the latter beat a hasty retreat to the north.

IMPROBABLE JOURNEYS

Something about BC encouraged an assortment of adventurers to set out on improbable journeys (see *Northern Adventure*, page 138). For many of those, the mountains were the ultimate challenge. In 1912, in the very early days of automobile travel, the Canadian Highway Association sponsored a 6,700-kilometre, cross-Canada trip to be attempted in a Reo motorcar by journalist Thomas Wilby—the car's owner—a driver, and a "mechanician." At that time, the Reo company was a serious contender in the car-manufacturing stakes, named for Ransom E. Olds, one of the original principals in the company that became Oldsmobile. He lost the right to use his surname when he left the original Olds company and started a new firm, naming it with his initials. He claimed this 1912 touring car was the best car he could build.

It was certainly good enough to make the first trans-Canada automobile trip, though the expedition had to make one detour into Washington State because BC roads were impassable. The men were feted in Chilliwack when they arrived, and photographed as they left for New Westminster. "Mr. Wilby gave the Free Press man a very interesting interview," reported the Chilliwack paper.

Instead of telling readers about any of the exciting events of the trip, the *Free Press* stodgily concluded that "Mr. Wilby stated that he had every courtesy from the towns and cities through which he passed and while there had been difficulties and hardships there had also been a great deal of pleasure and satisfaction."[5] Perhaps Wilby was keeping the good details for his own report.

Ten years later, the Edmonton Automobile and Good Roads Association offered a prize to the first car to drive from Edmonton to Jasper, and the city of Victoria began a contest for the first car to cross the mountains and get to Victoria, presumably not all the way by road. Charles Neimeyer, no stranger to these improbable journeys, and Edmontonian Frank Silverstone set off on the trip. Their Overland car was packed with picks, shovels, axes, hammers, four twelve-foot ten-inch planks and several shorter planks, a complete set of tools and spare parts, two spare tires and a spare wheel, fifty gallons of gasoline and five gallons of oil. Their route included railway grades, active and otherwise, and tote (supply) roads.

From Jasper on, they had with them a mountain guide. They "bumped the ties" along the train tracks from Jasper to Lucerne, BC, then continued along an abandoned railway grade. Back onto the railway tracks, the wheels straddling the rails, then a tote road, then the rails, then a tote road, then eventually a real road down from Hope to Vancouver. They arrived in Vancouver "with blistered hands and sore muscles... they brushed and built miles of road, constructed 36 bridges... killed a 14-foot grizzly bear with a 303 rifle, and took 200 pictures... They drove... along precipices where the variation of a hair would have thrown them hundreds of feet to death."[6] When they got to Victoria on July 4, they received a gold medal for the first trans-Rockies journey by an all-Canadian route, though not one that others were eager to attempt. At the end they still had nine gallons of gasoline and more than three gallons of oil left.

While BC roads didn't get good publicity from the trip, the Overland auto did. Not that it helped: by the end of the decade, the name was no longer in use, replaced by the Willys brand.

INHOSPITABLE HOSPITAL

Not amusing at all was some of the treatment meted out to the province's immigrants, in particular to those from Asia. But some stories made it clear that not every British Columbian was viciously prejudiced. In 1918, a man described as "a Hindu resident of Giscome"—most immigrants from India were referred to as Hindus, despite the fact that they were probably Sikhs—was brought to the Prince George hospital for treatment of a broken leg suffered at the Giscome sawmill. The train that brought him was met by a local doctor and ambulance, and the man was hurried to hospital.

There, the matron adamantly refused to let him in because of his skin colour. The doctor called the mayor; the mayor went to the hospital and tried to reason with the matron. She was immovable. The wounded man was lying on a stretcher on the lawn "in an agony of pain." The matron relented slightly: the man could enter provided a male nurse—of which there were none—came with him, presumably to prevent the lily-white hands of any of her female nurses from touching him. The ambulance man then volunteered to take the injured man to his own home and care for him.

"Considerable indignation is being expressed," reported the paper.[7] The reporter felt constrained to say that the man had served in the British army, was cleanly attired and unusually intelligent—these factors presumably strengthening his case for proper care. An investigation was promised.

IT'S THE CUSTOMS

The terms used are certainly those of the 19th century when it comes to people from China, but the image portrayed by the Yale *Inland Sentinel* on July 14, 1881, is too amusing to omit:

> On the arrival of the steamship Victoria, our Collector, Mr. Clute, observed the Chinamen on board were beautifully shod, and his suspicions being aroused, the Celestials were carefully examined, when it was found they were desirous of importing a large quantity of new goods without paying duty. One son of the Flowery Kingdom was clothed in six coats, another had his legs swathed in silk scarfs, a third had overalls enough to clothe quite a number of his companions, and a fourth brought some very nice Japanese handkerchiefs in his trunks. They were required to pay the full duty on the whole of their new goods, and will probably inform their

friends who may honor this city with a visit, that fewer garments will suit this climate.

JAIL

In small towns, those who got government contracts to build or maintain roads, buildings or wharves were open to constant criticism, much of it deserved. The Bella Coola *Courier* of October 18, 1913, complained:

> Owens, Manson, McMullin, Macfarlane and Company, who are running the jail business, will not be able to furnish Bella Coola with a lock-up on contract time.
>
> Last Saturday, court was held in the constable's office with seating accommodation for five. Some witnesses were permitted to lean against the outside of the counter, packed into a space of about 8x5 feet. Good enough for Bella Coola.
>
> The new building when completed will not include a courtroom. But as the above-mentioned firm is composed of a lot of small men, what better can be expected.

JAILWARDS—IN COMFORT

With no police cars to provide transport for an accused man, enforcers of the law often had to rely on alternate methods of transportation. But one accused man demanded his rights—and his money. Here, Justice of the Peace Henry Fry writes to the attorney general in October of 1879:

> Sir:
> Mr. Beaumont has spoken to me about this a/e of $2.50

before and I always looked upon it as too ridiculous to entertain.

The facts are simply these. When Mr. B was committed by me he was at once handed over to the Constable who was to take him to Town by canoe. He said it was too far to walk to where he could get one and his horse was out on the Mountain and it was arranged that as I had a Horse there I should put it in his Wagon and drive him and the constable down to Cowichan. This was done and he wants to charge $2.50 for the use of his wagon which was taken simply for his own convenience and at the time he preferred going to Victoria at once (as he could get legal advice) to being placed in our Lock-up.

JUMPING BEANS

In pre-television days, people took what they could find for entertainment. In 1899, Rossland got a novel amusement, reported in the *Miner* on August 29:

In the window of Mr. J.W. Spring's jewelry store are a number of dancing beans. They are on a plate and jump about in a very lively manner as though endowed with life as in reality they are. These beans grow in the tropics. In April there is a fly called the jumping bean fly that deposits an egg in each blossom on the jumping bean bush. Each blossom develops into a pod which opens and ripens in July when out drop two seed beans and one jumping bean. The latter are said to be difficult to gather, for it rains almost incessantly during the time they are falling. Immediately on falling the jumping beans begin to travel and it is slow tedious work to find them as they get into rocky crevices and under grass and weeds. There is a little kicker inside of each bean and when he moves it causes the bean to move also. About March next the flies in these beans will have developed sufficiently to escape from the prison house. They will cut round holes and hinge them with cement; then they will emerge from the houses that have been their home so long and go forth in search of adventures. It is feared, however, unless Mr. Spring keeps the beans warm, during the long winter, that the little kickers that are now in them will freeze to death. In their native place the weather is warm and here they are, therefore, very susceptible to the cold.

JUMPING THE FREIGHT, ON AND OFF

Everyone knew about jumping the freight train during the 1930s Depression, but the practice has a longer history. The McBride *Journal* reported on April 16, 1915, that a freight train on its way out of Prince George had been boarded by a gang of men.

"Although it was thought that the crew cleared the train before it left the yards, several men were found on the cars when the train reached Shelly. The train crew ordered them off, and after leaving the cars, they threw rocks at the train crew. One of the brakemen was struck on the back of the head with a rock, which cut his scalp. He drew a gun and shot his assailant in the leg . . . The brakeman . . . was arrested and comes up for trial today."

The three men, so-called Austrians, were later convicted of interfering with a train, and sent to jail for two months when they refused to pay a $20 fine. The brakeman was released on bail.

JUST KIDDING

From the Victoria *Daily Colonist*, December 7, 1888:

Fanny Clark, wife of the Kansas Kid, was arraigned on a charge of disturbing the serenity of life on Douglas street, by screaming on the street. She acknowledged the offence, and said that she couldn't help it; she "got that way sometimes."

"Fined $5, to be forthwith paid," remarked his honor. The prisoner's husband, who is to answer to a charge of vagrancy on Saturday, immediately stepped forward and tossed a double eagle [$20 American] on the clerk's desk, with a ring that roused the court.

"Haven't you anything smaller?" enquired the clerk. "The Kid" scornfully disclaimed possession of any coin of less than $20. After everybody in the court, including the reporters, who naturally glared in wild surprise at the questioner, had been asked to change the coin, the clerk found $15 in his drawer, handed it to Clark, and he and his wife left the court together.

Chapter Five
Loathsome, Lulu, Madness and Moose

KANSAS KID KAPTURED

From the Victoria *Daily Colonist*, September 5, 1902 (see also page 110):

Victoria atmosphere is not healthy for gentry of the light-fingered order, at least so must think "Kansas Kid" a tough who landed here from the Sound steamer Wednesday afternoon. Detectives Perdue and McDonald, in the usual course of events, were on the dock and spotted the Kid as soon as he made his appearance—knew him to be one of the slickest of the slick in the line of safe cracking and other delectable accomplishments in the same line. "Kansas Kid" no doubt thought Victoria and its good people were his "meat," but the "Kansas Kid" has been forcibly reminded that Victoria's police know a thing or two.

. . . the local detectives recognized him almost immediately and never let him get out of their sight for any length of time—and he kept them on the go all night and yesterday the game was continued. Finally to ease the pressure the "Kid" was taken in charge last night and locked up on a charge of vagrancy, for however successful the noted crook had been shadowed the previous night and day there was no knowing what might happen the second night.

LEPERS

Many stories are told of the lepers, mostly of Chinese origin, who were sent to D'Arcy Island, off Victoria, to live out miserable lives in isolation, even though it had been proved by the 1870s that leprosy was only mildly contagious. One story in the Victoria *Daily Colonist* on August 30, 1899, though, reported a remarkable cure:

> Sanitary Officer Wilson, with Dr. Fraser and a number of other municipal officials, paid a visit to the leper lazaretto at Darcy Island a day or so ago, leaving supplies and finding the patients who were burned in the recent fire quite recovered from their injuries and boasting a new skin that shows no trace of their loathsome disease.

LET 'ER RIP

Steamships plied the waters of many British Columbia rivers, with rival companies often piling on steam to beat each other upriver. In the spring of 1904, the *Mount Royal* and the *Hazelton* raced up the Skeena, each captain determined to bring his boat into Hazelton first. The captain of the *Mount Royal* tried to crowd the *Hazelton* into the shallows, whereupon the captain of the *Hazelton* turned his ship to hit his rival amidships, throwing her up onto the beach. Left behind and livid, the *Mount Royal*'s captain hauled out his rifle and began shooting. The matter ended up in marine court, where both captains were reprimanded, and the case closed.

LOATHSOME DISEASE

The phrase "loathsome disease" referred generally to any probably fatal and possibly contagious disease; in British Columbia, it was often applied to smallpox or leprosy. It also referred to sexually transmitted diseases such as syphilis, and was definitely a moral judgment. Not to worry though: makers of various patent medicines were happy to declare that their potions could readily cure such loathsome diseases (see *Pills for All Ills*, page 156.) Some stories were less happy; the Victoria *British Colonist* reported on July 22, 1859:

> A Frenchman whose name I could not ascertain, committed suicide ... in a cabin on Union Bay, on the morning of the 6th, by shooting himself through the head. He was afflicted with loathsome disease, and had been often heard to declare that he wished he was dead. The miners held an inquest and a verdict of "death by suicide" was rendered.

LOCK ME UP

Many men pleaded with the court system to be released from jail. Few pleaded to be locked up. But this letter from the provincial secretary's office to the attorney general in 1875 was an exception:

> A Chinaman named Wong Wing fearing violence from his countrymen desires to be locked up in the gaol, that he may be in safety, until he has time to arrange with his creditors if this can be permitted. I shall feel obliged if you will give the necessary instruction to the Superintendent of Police.

LOVELY LULU

Lulu Sweet, ringlets dangling and looking not a day more than her sixteen years, was a great favourite of theatregoers in 1860s Victoria when she played there as part of a travelling troupe from San Francisco. Her acting was, they said, graceful, beautiful and impeccable, and her demeanour on- and offstage entrancing. When the troupe crossed Georgia Strait to play at a club erected for the entertainment of the Royal Engineers, those men were equally entranced. Commanding officer Colonel Richard Moody took the young lady for a sail around the coast and islands. When she asked the name of an island they passed, the colonel was exceedingly gracious. It had no name, he said, but now it does: we shall call it Lulu Island. And thus was named the island that is now a large part of Richmond and the site of the Vancouver International Airport.

LOWERY OF THE *LEDGE*—AND THE OTHER *LEDGE*, THE *PAYSTREAK*, AND THE *CLAIM*, AND THE *LEDGE* YET AGAIN

Five feet tall and colonel because he liked the title, Robert Thornton Lowery was BC's most colourful newspaperman. He was verbose, funny, frequently drunk and often smoking a cigar, and passionate about the rights of the worker, whether miner or prostitute. Editor at various times of the Kaslo *Claim*, the Sandon *Paystreak*, the New Denver *Ledge*, the Greenwood *Ledge* and the Nakusp *Ledge*, he cut a writerly swath through the mining towns of the West Kootenay from the 1890s though the first decade of the 20th century. His enemies were anyone and, more often, any big business, that he saw as preying on the common man. The Canadian Pacific Railway was a frequent target, as were capitalists of any description. The CPR was so affronted by his frequent criticism that it refused to let his newspapers on board, and gave him a ticket, not to ride, but to stride, along the railbed.

He started his first BC newspaper, the Kaslo *Claim*, in 1893; it lasted thirteen weeks. "Busted, By Gosh," read the inscription on the tombstone he printed on the front page, "Sacred to the memory of the Kaslo Claim. Let Her R.I.P." He suggested the paper's supporters would be sad to see him go, but its enemies would be enabled to "bamboozle the public without any fear of being molested, and consequently they will be happy." He ran paid-up ads correctly, but those in arrears were printed upside down or sideways.

He moved on to other papers, but was often broke, as advertising and subscription revenues ran behind expenses. "In one way we are ahead of other Kootenay editors," he wrote from New Denver in 1899. "We have enough of wood on hand to last until 1900. This is about the only thing we are long on. We are short on cash, and job work, while mint juleps, boiled shirts and diamonds are only visible to us when we dream of the rosy past. Thus do things grow serious and serve to teach us that in the midst of life we are in the soup, or New Denver."

When one mining town went bust, he moved on to another that was booming. Of his battle to keep newspapers going, he once wrote, "A parson in the east prayed for lightning to strike a brewery in his town, and the event recently occurred. Years ago a parson in New Denver prayed for rain, and it has rained more or less ever since. We have often prayed for our delinquent subscribers to dig up, and many have never dug. We wish the parson who knocked out the brewery would take them in hand. We would divide the results with him."

He was as likely to pen a tongue-in-cheek "New Rules of Whist," detailing the worst practices he saw at the card table, as to write a tirade against the malefactors of whatever town he found himself in. A bit of a dandy, he sported a neat goatee and wore steel-rimmed glasses. He couldn't leave the bottle alone, and was, on occasion, admitted to hospital when his drinking knocked him down. He died of that quaint old complaint, dropsy—excess fluid buildup, probably caused by his drinking—in 1921, at the age of 62.

LYNCHING

The horrors of American lynchings, usually but not always of blacks in the American South, were often front-page news in BC. Every once in a while, though, BC had its own version of lynching. In 1859, the *Daily Colonist* reported that a Nanaimo Justice of the Peace had ordered an Indian who was accused of a felony tied up and brutally flogged, without trial and within an hour of the man's arrest. And the paper cited other cases where the same JP had anticipated Gilbert and Sullivan: first the punishment, then the trial.

Other attempts at lynching were stopped just in time. The Victoria *Daily Colonist* reported one such case on November 2, 1894:

> On October 1, a man named Currie eloped from Mission City with his landlady, a Mrs. Ross. They took with them some $600 of Mr. Ross' money. They have been traced from place to place for sometime, until rounded up at Blaine. Currie is now in jail at New Westminster.
>
> It transpires that Currie, who ran away with Mrs. Ross and her six children, was captured near Blaine by a lynching party, and narrowly escaped death. The lynching party were rowing with the prisoner to a spot near Blaine to do violence to Currie when the boat came into Canadian waters, and Ross, the outraged husband, who had been made a special constable by the magistrate, demanded the custody of the prisoner in the name of the Queen, thus saving Currie's life. Currie was a butcher and among the many things he stole was a live cow to provide for his inamorata and her six children.

MAD AUSTRIANS

Just before the First World War, there seemed to be a sudden surge in the number of "mad Austrians" around the province, presumably immigrants from the Austro-Hungarian Empire. In Prince Rupert in 1911, for example, the headline writer resorted to mad alliteration: "Apparition in An Airy Attire; Austrian Apparently Almost Asphyxiated Attracted Attention." The Austrian in question, reported the Prince Rupert *News*, had forgotten to open his hotel room window a little to let in fresh air. "The gentleman, who it is whispered, is distantly connected with his national nobility, had an overpowering inclination to cool his fevered brow, and other portions of his anatomy, in the fresh breezes of night." So out he went, clad in his nightshirt, so enchanted with the evening that he indulged in "a few light fantastic evolutions on tip-toes." And then came the minion of the law. The dancer, having no good explanation, was lodged in Chief Vickers' "hotel."[1]

Half a province away, in Nelson, also in 1911, a "mad Austrian prisoner" made a sensational escape from custody by jumping from the window of an express train. He was arrested, but escaped once more, this time from jail.

MAD MOOSE

How did the moose cross the river? Not always by swimming. Steamboat captain John Bonser recounted that, while his ship was loading wood on a narrow, swiftwater reach of the Stikine, a huge bull moose calmly walked aboard, perhaps seeing the boat as a convenient bridge. Not so easy: the moose got his antlers caught in the cargo and proceeded to bellow and thrash about, kicking the bulkhead to splinters. How to get him out? Genealogist Roger Knowles Thompson had this story from the family of the steamboat captain: "One man devised an answer. He formed a noose and managed to slip it over those parts which are the essence of male moosely pride." When the crew on shore hauled on the rope, the moose obeyed the summons. The ship left an hour later with the moose still furiously bawling onshore.[2]

MADDER MOOSE

Moose and trains don't mix well, especially in the winter. What better place for a moose to meander when the snow is two metres deep than down a nicely cleared train track? Of course, it's not that easy to get out of a snowy ravine, a truth that moose continue to discover in the 21st century. From the McBride *Journal*, April 28, 1917:

> There was about ten feet of snow on the level between Rooney and Giscombe, a fact that made it hard going for the moose, and as soon as they floundered through snow to the railway track they liked to keep within the snow walls on either side. A moose had not very much regard for the right-of-way of the trains on the track, and on

several occasions the trains had to be stopped so that the animals, which had paid no regard to the engine, might be chased off by the train crew. Although great care was taken, six or seven moose were actually killed, but all because they insisted on daring the engine to mortal combat. They got very annoyed when they discovered that they were being chased down the snow valley, and after putting up with it for a couple of miles, would turn and charge the engine. This usually resulted fatally. Two moose which picked a fight with the snow plow were luckier. They ran ahead of the plow for about two miles, finally turned and charged right into the rotary plow. The plow picked them up and threw them about fifty feet from the track, but they were seen to pick themselves up and move off apparently uninjured.

MAMMOTHS AND MONSTERS

Monster stories were always popular, especially in the north when excitement was in short supply. On occasion, editors tied themselves into semantic knots, with a nudge-nudge, wink-wink intelligible only to those who already knew the story. In May of 1899, the Bennett *Sun* reported the discovery of a 20-foot serpent. The reptile was described, as the men who had rushed to the scene stood at the head of its cave, by "a huge medical man of Atlin."

"This creature," the doctor is reported to have said, "is unclassified, and tho' in general it has somewhat the appearance of a large serpent it also has marked characteristics peculiar to itself." The head and tail, he declared, were like those of a marten, "especially the piercing eye and peculiarly shaped nose."[3]

The crowd turned raucous, as they suggested this and that, each according to their nature: the liquor dealer, the steamboat man, the US citizen. And then the story continued ever more wildly, showing itself as a satire on the people, the government and the newspapers of the day—inspired, it would seem, by some article in the far-away Victoria *Daily Colonist*. The beast had served its purpose.

Three decades later, the Stewart newspaper was on the trail of another mammoth monster. Ice worms do, of course, exist: some have seen hundreds of these tiny blind black creatures, a centimetre or two long, emerge onto the surface of glaciers as night falls. But mammoth ice worms? Well, perhaps in Robert Service's country... or in the bar. From the Portland Canal *News*, May 6, 1927:

> A number of intrepid spirits among the hardy explorers and prospectors of the camp are eagerly awaiting the opening of transportation on the Marmot in order that they may go in to the north fork and try to get a line on "Garbevoo," the mammoth ice worm that attacked Harold Garden last fall while he was attending to his own business of surveying the Marmot mineral claims.
>
> These seasoned veterans, well cheered by a winter spent in comfortable chairs and more-or-less-so-bunks figure that if they can induce the beast to come out of his hole they will have a good excuse for coming back to town, lingering another two weeks before going back and trying to trap him—or doing something else again.

MAMMOTH MUSHROOMS

Huge mushrooms were always good for a few column inches. From the Victoria *Daily British Colonist* on October 27, 1879:

A mammoth mushroom measuring over nine inches in diameter was exhibited in the show window of the Arcade oyster saloon yesterday afternoon. The cryptogamic grew in ground in the vicinity of the Gorge Hotel.

A MAN, A PLAN, A CANAL

BC's topography is daunting, its mountains forming rocky barriers, its rainforest almost impenetrable at times, its rivers swift and narrow and often deadly. But where some see trouble, others, dreamers and schemers by nature, see opportunity. William Adolph Baillie Grohman was one such dreamer, an Anglo-Austrian who counted Teddy Roosevelt among his hunting pals and who was enchanted by the Kootenay region when he first saw it in the early 1880s.

He found particularly interesting the streambeds of the Columbia and Kootenay rivers, which rise very close together in the southern Rockies, then take opposite paths—the Columbia flowing north, the Kootenay south—until they rejoin half a province away. Baillie Grohman inspected the river courses, and also looked carefully at the flats near present-day Creston, at the head of Kootenay Lake, inundated every spring by the flooding waters of the Kootenay. If, he said, the Kootenay could be diverted into the Columbia via a short canal, floods could be averted and rich farmland created on the flats. And if he owned the flatland, he could sell it for a pretty penny and be rich, as well as creating something very worthwhile.

In fact, later dyking and diversions did create rich farmland. But Baillie Grohman's plans were much more grandiose, akin to those of other river-diverters in the 20th century who envisioned hydro dams—which did come to pass—and fresh-water-for-the-Americans schemes—which did not.

Baillie Grohman did convince the BC government that his plan had merit, and was promised large land grants if he brought the scheme to fruition. But the Canadian Pacific Railway was opposed, believing the change in water levels on the Columbia would engulf its rail tracks. The CPR argued that diverting rivers was a federal responsibility; like many other subsequent plans, Baillie Grohman's was scuppered by the federal-provincial divide. Baillie Grohman had to install locks on his canal to control water flow, making the canal useless for its original purpose. Nonetheless, he built on, using Chinese labourers to construct a ditch fourteen metres wide, more than 2,000 metres long, three metres deep. Only two boats ever passed through the canal. The second one damaged the locks and rendered them virtually unusable. The canal was eventually filled in.

MARITAL MANOEUVRES

Swiftwater Bill was a marryin' man—though perhaps he overdid it, rushing to the altar four times. Best known for making a fortune in the Klondike, and then losing it playing pool, the dapper dandy first married music hall artiste Gussie LaMore in 1897, after buying up all the eggs in Dawson—or so it is said—after he saw another man buying her fried eggs, the most expensive item on the menu. He either had them all fried and fed them to dogs, or gave them all to Gussie. Whichever, it worked and Gussie married him, but the pair soon separated.

His marital history is tangled from then on. A *New York Times* article in 1898 says his wife was willing to divorce him if she got $25,000, though she knew he would immediately marry her sister, Belle LaMore. A few years later, he caught up with Gussie, and planned to remarry her, but redisappeared with Belle.

A year or two later, Swiftwater Bill—actual name Bill Gates—was watching Gussie dance at a Victoria dance hall when 16-year-old Bera Beebe caught his eye. The two "kept company," then went to Seattle with Bera's mother. Bera and Bill eloped, the mother chased them down, the couple was thrown in jail—but the mother relented, perhaps with the aid of a large donation, and the two were wed.

Bill abandoned Bera in 1903, marrying a seventeen-year-old, even though he was not in fact divorced. Bera agreed to divorce him in 1904, occasioning headlines in Victoria as well as many other places across the continent. Bera's mother, who had had him jailed for bigamy, but had bailed him out and pawned her diamonds to send him north to seek another fortune, later wrote his biography, in which, it seems, all had been forgiven.

MARRIAGE MAYBE

Then, as now, beautiful blondes knew their price and their power—and had their problems. A woman by the name of Eva Wilson left her live-in lover but he tried to bring her back by force, as reported in the Victoria *Daily Colonist*, February 4, 1885:

> A Daily Colonist reporter visited Mrs McDonald, or Eva Wilson, as she prefers to be called, in her room, at the

Magnolia House, last evening. The truant wife was found to be a very beautiful blond about 22 years of age. She has a slight German accent, and was attired in a long sealskin, which she was in the act of removing when the reporter entered. In reply to a query she stated that she was never married to McDonald, but had lived with him for several months as his wife . . . He had frequently requested that they should be married, and she had informed him that she would become his bride on receipt of $10,000; that she did not love him, but would be faithful to him if he would accede to her business proposition. About six weeks ago she accompanied him to this city, and while dining at the Lick House he acted so brutally towards her that she was obliged to leave him. She also stated that she first met him in a Victoria bagnio, where she had lived for two years. The attempted abduction on Sat night she characterized as a brutal outrage, and vowed to have her assailants punished.

MARRIAGE PROPOSALS

From the Zeballos *Miner*, February 27, 1939:

Dear Editor:

Will you please place my request on the front page of your newspaper.

Wont someone whom has struck it rich please write to me. I have blonde hair and blue eyes, pass for 35 yrs. Old, 5 foot 1 inch tall, weigh 124 pounds, a commercial education; I have been married but no children. I will marry the one whom will give me three thousand dollars.

I will then fly to him, and we could marry, he must have means. I would love to live in BC I will answer all letters if he sends a stamp.

Please send my photo back. I prefer a man over 40 yrs. Old; I have no children , thanks in advance. Hester Owens, Box 268, Room 706, Rives Bldg., Los Angeles, Calif.

Her picture may be seen at the Miner.

MERRILY, MERRILY, MERRILY ... OOPS

Not all of BC's "cowboys" rode horses. Young, male and often ignorant of the power of nature, miners, railway builders and assorted immigrants frequently got into trouble through ill-considered decisions. One such account appeared in the Yale *Inland Sentinel* on December 9, 1880:

A few irrepressible resolute workmen ... took it into their venturesome heads that if the steamers never came, they could navigate the Fraser river themselves. Accordingly, a small flat-bottomed boat was hurriedly built, a stock of provisions packed away, and tool chests reckoned on for ballast, the word given 'all aboard' sarted the distinguished navigators Wednesday morning. Away they went with the swift current passing Yale, and all was serene as

Capt. P. struck up Tom Moore's gay 'Canadian Boat Song,' and 'the waters seemed to stray and glide like happiness away,' the surroundings reminding one of the couplet,

'Though much he fret and chafe and toil,
Till all his eddying currents boil.'

Reaching the vicinity of Emory the lookout discovered piles of ice ahead which, comparatively speaking, made mole-hills look mountains—and freeze, as it were, the blood in the veins of the brave mariners—but every nerve was bent to duty and a splurge made for the shore amid the agonizing cry of, 'pull, boys, pull for the shore'! Fortunately the frail craft was got into the eddy and pretty soon an effort was made to haul her out upon the ice lining the shore. No sooner was the boat and men upon the ice than down the luckless boat went to her natural element and the now unhappy men to their middles in the cruely cold Fraser. Not relishing the situation an other gallant effort speedily brought the whole party safe to the welcome beach. After hanging around a glowing fire congratulating and consoling each other for an hour, (we have not heard of any thanksgiving for deliverance from a watery grave,) our shipwrecked heroes strengthened themselves with creature comforts and journeyed along the road towards the hospitable quarters of Yale, where many stories are now related by 'experienced voyagers' of the perils of the deep. This case ought to be a warning to those who may feel inclined to set the blockades of Jack-frost at defiance and a roving go where no open channel exists. 'All's well that ends well.'

MORE MARITAL MISERY

Marital deception and heartbreak, tragedy and bloodshed, are not 21st century inventions. In 1888, Michael Kennedy went to Golden with his wife, where they ran a ranch. A man named Archer began visiting their house while Kennedy was away. "Kennedy, who was insanely jealous, when he believed his wife was unfaithful, and that Archer was the man in the case, lay in wait for Archer and shot him." Kennedy was arrested, found guilty and sentenced to life imprisonment.

"When Kennedy was sentenced he jumped up in the dock and began cursing the police and authorities, and there was quite a scene in the court, It took about eight men to shackle him and literally drag him through the streets of Kamloops to the jail."

Kennedy's wife divorced him and married a second time. Kennedy was released through the king's clemency in 1902.[4]

MORGUE MUTTERINGS

From the Victoria *Daily Colonist*, August 10, 1895:

Dr. Crompton said he desired to call attention to the disgraceful condition of the morgue. When he made his post mortem examination of the body he was continually annoyed by the children and other persons, who persisted in looking through the windows of the building, which are low enough to the ground to permit of this being done. When he first reached the morgue he found numbers of children collected there. And directly he entered he heard one boy ask another outside if he had seen the corpse. The other boy replying in the negative, the first lad told him to step up on a box and look in at the window. This state of things Dr. Crompton said he stopped at once. The last time he went to the morgue to perform a post mortem, he not only found people looking in at the windows, but the door was open, and anyone who liked could enter. He was told by the caretaker of the market, that though the morgue was not under his charge, he had several times sent children away from the place.

MOSQUITOES

Mosquitoes were the bane of everyone's—and every horse's—life in the early days of the colony and province. Charles Wilson, working on the boundary survey in 1862, was eloquent about the torment he experienced in the Fraser Valley, in the days before swamps were drained and dykes built. He cursed what he called a small biting gnat, "it gets through the mosquito curtains & its sting is very venomous. At present, my skin is something like a leopard, all spotted."[5] The following year, he was back near Chilliwack, and railing again at the ever-present bugs. "It is perfect agony performing even the regular actions of life," he wrote. "Washing is a perfect torture, they settle *en masse* upon you perfectly covering every portion of the body exposed." The mosquitoes so tormented one of the group that he opened a vein in his neck with his scratching, became very weak from loss of blood and could hardly stand up.

The local natives tried to help Wilson by painting him with vermilion; though he appreciated the assistance, he thought his appearance highly amusing. But, he said, his hands were so swollen and stiff he could barely use them and had to wrap them in wet towels before he could work. "Even when wearing kid gloves the bites through the needle holes were sufficient to produce this. Each mule, as it is packed is obliged to be led in a circle of fires continually kept up, as they are quite intractable when worried by the mosquitoes; two of Darah's mules have been blinded & 6 of our horses were so reduced we had to turn them out on the prairie & let them take their chances of living. I never saw anything like the state of their skins, one mass of sores." Their tents were so covered with the infuriating insects that the canvas was all but invisible. The overall effect was that several of the men looked years older, the doctor's hair was turning grey, and Wilson thought some of them might go quite mad.[6]

Things weren't much better in the Kootenays in the 1880s. J.A. Lees and W.J. Clutterbuck described their experience when they were put ashore on the banks of the Columbia by a steamer and were soon "being literally eaten by the most awful mosquitoes it has ever been our lot to meet or be meat for. We had to repel the attacks of countless millions of mosquitoes . . . and through it all remember the thermometer stood at about 90 in the shade, with never a breath of wind to alleviate our sufferings from the heat.

"People at home read of sandflies, Cingalese leeches, stinging ants, mosquitoes, and the like, and the fashion is to treat all such matters more or less as jokes, and to affect merriment at the idea of getting well bitten by any of them, but the truth is that there is no misery on earth equal to a really bad attack of these demons. We all thought we had seen mosquitoes before, in Norway, in India, and in the States, but until now we knew nothing absolutely nothing of the concentrated essence of torture that they are capable of inflicting when you invade their real home."

Though they had brought gauze to put over their hats and faces, mosquitoes swarmed onto the gauze and kept them from seeing and breathing; they took the veils off, replacing them only when they could endure the biting no longer.

"At last finding a place where the tall gaunt stems of the burnt forest gave a little more chance of light and air, we cleared a very uncomfortable patch just big enough for the tent, cooked some bacon and made tea, and then huddled under our blankets as the only possible asylum from the ever-increasing levies of our relentless enemies. For as the sun went down a new and more formidable variety came upon the scene: in fact we soon found that each period of the day had its own particular detachment, every new one appearing to be more insatiable than the last. Unfortunately the arrival of a fresh contingent did not induce those already on the spot to desist from their labours."[7]

MOTHERS-IN-LAW

Many men have complained about their wives' mothers, leading to the endless mother-in-law jokes—though some might suggest it would be appropriate to have an equal number of son-in-law jokes. But few sons-in-law have gone to the length of writing to the attorney general to try to solve their problem. In 1896, one resident of Peardonville, a hamlet near Abbotsford, made that extraordinary effort. There is no record of his success or failure.

Dear Sir:

Would you kindly inform me if I can find any way of getting my wife from staying with my mother-in-law, we have been married for (3) three years and all my troubles have been caused by my wife's mother. She has influenced my wife to hurt my feelings and she is being led astray by her mother talking to her. I would ask you one more question if you please. We have got one baby girl 2 years old. And my wife's mother will not even allow me to take her for a walk for even a few minutes and the child is being permitted to say things which I as her father or any other person with common sense would not have her to say and If my wife will not leave her present abode and go and live with me I would like to have the custody of our only child. Hoping you will give me favourable reply. I remain Dear Sir Yours Resp., Edward Thompson

Chapter Six
Necromancers, Opium Smugglers and Not Dead Yet

NECROMANCY

Magic and mayhem were an irresistible combination on the stages of the 19th century: present a lot of illusion, a little blood (tomato ketchup, maybe? Or animal blood?) and a hint of sex and the audience was thrilled almost to death, though preferably not their own. How times don't change.

In December of 1873, Bosco, described as the great necromancer and illusionist, came back to Victoria after a two-year tour of the United States. "He returns with many new and startling feats which he acquired while East," revealed the *Daily Colonist*, "and among other acts will perform the Hindoo Basket Trick, in which a young girl of this city will assist him. This remarkable feat consists in placing the girl in a basket and passing a sword through the middle of the basket. Cries of pain and streams of blood issue from the receptacle; all present begin to believe a real tragedy has been enacted when the girl is produced without a scratch. The Professor has billed the town with gorgeous placards which... are an ornament to the dead walks and fences... Price of admission has been fixed at 50 cents."[1]

In May of 1892, Victoria's small coloured community advertised some necromancy of their own. "Colored society excited," ran the advertisement, "The cake walking craze has struck us!"[2] Among the attractions of the "colored jubilee" were dancers, singers, musicians including an African band, grand calcium light effects, and, of course, necromancers.

Necromancy, though now taken to mean predicting the future through communication with the dead, was a great catch-all term in the 19th century. Whatever its meaning, Bishop Edward Cridge, dean of Christ Church in Victoria, had no doubt of its evil nature. He preached against "Spiritualism, or Modern Necromancy" as "a very ancient wickedness."[3] He had his sermon printed for the benefit of those who might have been tempted, declaring "no spirits of the dead hover around the living to terrify or cheer or intreat them."

He was fighting something of a losing battle, for spiritualism had a wide following. Victoria photographer Hannah Maynard, for example, created photos showing departed spirits, and was a great devotee of séances and other spiritualist endeavours. Mediums found good business in Victoria as well as other towns in the province. Even the founder of the Vancouver *Sun* was fascinated by the idea of spiritualism, and the Freemasons were very interested in the occult during the 19th century. Fierce battles were waged in the letters to the editor and editorial columns of newspapers over the possible truth or possible deviltry of spiritualism.

Necromancer Herrmann the Great travelled around British Columbia theatres in the 1890s. Black arts, sorcery, legerdemain and the supernatural formed part of his act. "Hermann's masterpiece was Strobeika," reported the *Daily Colonist*.[4] "An assistant was locked to the board by a committee of gentlemen from the audience. Yale locks were used, and the keys retained by the committee." The curtains were drawn, then drawn back, and a young lady appeared strapped to the board, with the assistant coming to the stage from the street. After

Herrmann's death, his wife, Adelaide Herrmann, continued her dances, "the most dazzling and bewildering ever seen," with thousands of coloured lights and voluminous and ever-moving draperies.⁵

In the Okanagan, land developer John Moore Robinson founded Summerland, Peachland and Naramata, boosting them all as new Edens where gentleman farmers could live in sunshine and happiness, sustained by the ample products of fertile land. Naramata was his favourite. He had planned to call the town Brighton Beach, naming it for the hometown of his family in England.

But Robinson was heavily involved in spiritualism, and truly believed that the denizens of the spirit world could speak to him. A Mrs. Gillespie, wife of the postmaster, was a medium in the American Spiritualistic Church. At a séance one night, she spoke with the voice of a Sioux chief named Big Moose, who talked about his wife with love and said she was named Naramattah, the smile of Manitou. Between them, Gillespie and Robinson decided this would be a fine name for the infant town.

NORTHERN ADVENTURE

Call them adventurers or charlatans, visionaries or fools, BC has had more than its share of people—most of them men, but some women—who found here the larger canvas on which they could paint their dreams. And the north, with its wide reaches of virtually unpopulated territory, its forests, and its seeming air of romantic adventure, was a strong draw for such characters.

Among them was Charles Bedaux, a man for whom the word quixotic might have been invented. Bedaux was born in France in 1887 and emigrated to the United States some twenty years later. He invented a time-management system that made him rich; he was loved by management and hated by unions. He was a Nazi sympathizer and a friend of the Duke of Windsor who had abdicated as king of Britain to marry the divorced woman he loved. He may have passed on information from American firms that employed him to the German government before and during the Second World War.

In 1932, he came to northern Alberta to hunt ducks. Two years later, he was back again, this time with a huge entourage and a plan to forge a path across the Rockies to the Pacific at the mouth of the Stikine River, possibly as some kind of military route.

With him were his wife, Fern; her friend—some say Bedaux's mistress—the elusive, titian-haired Bilonha Chiesa; Fern's maid, Josephine; Bedaux's Scottish gamekeeper; a Citroën mechanic; and award-wining cinematographer Floyd Crosby, of *High Noon* fame, who was to document the expedition. BC surveyor Frank Swannell, a phalanx of 50 cowboys, guides, axemen, and even a professional skier, as well as 130 horses and 20 tonnes of equipment and supplies, including French novels, cases of champagne, cans of truffles, silk pyjamas, and fancy dinnerware were part of the expedition. One pack horse was dedicated to carrying Fern's shoes.

Automaker Citroën donated five nickel-plated, half-track trucks (wheels in front, Caterpillar tracks at the back) of a type already tested through Africa and across Asia in mammoth trips known as the Croisières Noire and Jaune.

Bedaux, his trucks and his pack train left Edmonton in July of 1934, and were greeted by cheering crowds and civic dinners in every town from there to Fort St. John, their money very welcome in this dark Depression year. But it didn't take long for problems to appear. The trucks, vastly overloaded with supplies, broke down constantly, got just two miles to a gallon of gas, and were almost useless in the infamously deep Peace River gumbo. Finally, it was decided to abandon them after the expedition left Fort St. John.

The cameraman wanted a spectacular scene, and Bedaux was glad to oblige. Two of the trucks would be dispatched over the edge of a steep cliff to plummet into the river below, while a third would disappear downriver on a raft. One gunshot would notify the cameramen to start filming; a second would tell the drivers to start their engines and push the trucks toward the precipice. But Bedaux's fox terrier was terrified by the second shot, leaped into the front truck and bit the driver when he tried to throw it out.

"Meantime, I had started #2 in compound low, and jumped out as pre-arranged," recounted expedition member Bruce Bocock, "when to my horror, I saw it creeping up to John who hadn't started #1. Fortunately, I got #2 shut off again before it pushed John over the bank, but from that point on, John had little use for fox terriers."[6] Eventually, the trucks were sent over the edge, and the cameramen got their shots.

The expedition continued on with horses and mules, through mud and rain, heat and mosquitoes. Bedaux grew increasingly autocratic, complaining his tents were not ready for him when he arrived each evening, leaving crippled horses behind him on the trail, departing from camp before the horses were packed. "This is the sort of thing you must be prepared to put up with when you pack a millionaire through the wilderness," Bocock commented wryly. Meanwhile, the ladies dallied for hours every morning, preparing themselves to face the day, and the movie crew provided comic relief, setting up scenes of fire and desperation to make their filming more dramatic.

It was ever more difficult to find feed for the horses, wolves stalked the pack train, and the group went 31 days without fresh meat until someone finally shot a moose. At the end of September, almost 12 weeks into the trip and, according to Swannell's calculations, more than 400 kilometres from Telegraph Creek and the Stikine River, Bedaux ordered the group to turn back.

At Fort Grahame on the Finlay River, they hired five freight canoes and ran the lakes and rivers back down to Hudson's Hope. They then rode trucks to Pouce Coupe, and took the train to Edmonton. The Bedaux Sub-Arctic Expedition was over.

Before it started, a reporter had asked Bedaux why. "It's fun to do things others consider impossible," he replied. When he returned, he seemed not at all subdued. "I'll be back," he promised—but then the real drama of his life intervened.

He had become an American citizen in 1917, and, in 1943, the Americans arrested him for conspiring with the enemy. He committed suicide in a Miami jail in 1944—or, if you are an advocate of conspiracy theories, was murdered to prevent him from revealing the truth about the wartime activities of prominent American industrialists.

NOT DEAD YET

In June of 1894, the *Kootenay Mail* of Revelstoke ragged the editor of the Nakusp *Ledge*, which had reported the drowning death of three men in Trout Lake: "The three men are still alive and kicking, and

'Scotty' and Treanor send a letter from Trout Lake declining to be killed off... The compensating feature of being drowned and disposed of in that manner is that one's debts are left behind... Still, everything else aside, it must be very awkward for a man to be accounted dead and buried..." Then with great glee, the *Mail* man reproduces the account of the drowning, suggesting that the writer could be compared to Rider Haggard.

"Their cabin was situated on cleared ground some distance back from the river. About three o'clock on the Monday morning, when all the men were in bed, they were startled by hearing the large stones which composed the fireplace being thrown against the wooden bunks in which they were sleeping. Before they could make any attempt to get up the cabin collapsed and in a moment the occupants were struggling in the icy, rushing water. Hoar and Stewart were thrown against a log, which they grasped and clung to until washed out into the lake. Treanor and Metcalf must have been struck by timber in the mad rush of water, as they were not seen again. Hoar and 'Scotty' held on to the log for some time, until the latter was crushed against it by the end of another log. He disappeared with the words, 'Good-bye, Billy; I can't hold on any longer.' Hoar managed to get ashore after a while, but not before he had suffered serious injuries from the buffetting of the driftwood.

The bodies were recovered the next day and buried at Trout Lake."[7]

Which was undoubtedly a great surprise to the still-living men. The *Mail* editor didn't suggest it, but perhaps legendary *Ledge* editor Robert Lowery was, not unusually for him, writing after having imbibed a little too much. Or perhaps a good story is too much to resist, true or not.

NOT DEAD YET, II

From the Alice Arm *Herald*, May 23, 1931:

> The many Anyox friends of Bob Salter who was reported dead at Halifax a short time ago will be pleased to learn he is very much alive. In reply to a letter of enquiry, Frank Hill received a telegram from Mr. Salter himself on Tuesday which was as follows:
>
> "Please give me all information in letter, have had several letters like yours these last five weeks but cannot account for any of them. Say hello to all the boys as I am still alive."

NOT DEAD YET, III

In the early days of Prince Rupert, boardwalks were laid atop the banks that bordered the streets, which were little more than dank and muddy ravines. One night, the undertaker's helper hefted a dead man on his back to take him from his cabin down to the undertaking parlour. The trek was long and the boardwalk slippery. The helper lost his footing and tumbled into the ravine, losing his burden en route. No matter: he scrambled around until he found the body, loaded it up once more, and headed on to his destination, where he slung the man onto the slab. But wait: when the doctor arrived to officially pronounce death, he exclaimed instead, "This man's not dead! He's drunk." And he was right. The undertaker took up a lantern and went back along the boardwalk—finally finding the actual corpse in the ravine. History does not record what happened to the drunk.[8]

NOT JUST BC BUD, EH?
THE OPIUM SMUGGLERS OF VICTORIA

Victoria was the talk of the town from the *New York Times* to the Auburn *Weekly* in 1888. It wasn't the sea air or the lovely flowers making the news, but a "well organized syndicate of opium smugglers." Run by the shadowy C.J. Joslyn, also known as Boss Harris, the syndicate was said to have agents all along the American border, smuggling Victoria-manufactured opium into the United States in every nefarious way they could devise.

Though smoking opium was not illegal in the United States at the time, importing it directly from China was, and any opium arriving from elsewhere was heavily taxed. Smuggling opium over the border from Canada, where importing, possession, manufacture and sale were legal, was therefore very profitable. Joslyn/Harris, who seems to have been unknown in Victoria although the newspaper stories declared him a Victoria resident, was described as "immensely rich."

"He makes no effort to conceal the fact that he is the biggest smuggler of opium in the Dominion . . . The value of the combined product of the factories in BC—the headquarters of the Harris gang—is estimated at $5,000,000 per annum, and of this more than 90 percent goes to the United States."[9] Boss Harris's share of the profits was said to be $30,000 of the $100,000 in US duty avoided on every run.

In 1888, 13 factories in Victoria's Chinatown processed raw opium that arrived on ships from China. One such factory was located behind today's City Hall, and had more than 30 employees. Very little of the processed drug was sold in Canada; most was smuggled south, an estimated 50 tons of opium leaving Victoria every year.

Many gangs and, occasionally, independent smugglers, took opium across the line. In December of 1888, Michigan detectives waylaid Captain Harry Durant, a man they called the head of one opium-smuggling gang, "standing 10 feet away and firing 20 shots at him in rapid succession." They missed; Durant escaped.

Adding insult to injury, Durant later gave an interview to an American reporter from where he and a good friend and fellow smuggler were "living in good style . . . [at] the swell hotel of the town [Sarnia, Ontario]." The reporter recounted how opium was brought from the Victoria factories to Sarnia, then smuggled across the river to the US—sometimes in tin cans in the smugglers' coat pockets—then traded on to San Francisco and other cities. In 1889, the *New York Times* reported the capture in Tacoma, Washington, of "Black Bill" Easton and gang chief Jack Powers, as well as a railway conductor. "For several years," sad the *Times*, "the Puget Sound country has been infested with an organized gang of opium smugglers, with headquarters at Victoria, BC. Although inspectors have been constantly patrolling the border and searching all incoming steamers, only a few of these smugglers have been overhauled, and those captured proved to be nothing but stool pigeons for the leaders of the gang."

The trade ended in 1908, when a law was passed in Canada making illegal the possession of opium for sale or trafficking; it also forbade the importing and manufacture of the drug for non-medical reasons. By 1911, further legislation made any possession or use of opium illegal.

ON TRACK—OR NOT

Railway companies came in for a great deal of ribbing as customers analyzed their service, or lack of same. The Pacific Great Eastern, sometimes known as "the railway from nowhere to nowhere" since it went from Squamish to Quesnel, took the brunt of the teasing. It was dubbed the Please Go Easy or the Prince George Eventually. But the Prince George *Citizen* took on another railway company on May 28, 1911:

> Some travelers were discussing the meaning of O.T. placed after the arrival of the passenger trains. One of them who seemed to know more about trains than anyone else said that on the G.T.P. "O.T." means On Time, on the C.P.R. it means On the Track and on the C.N.R. it means Off the Track.

OPPRESSED, BUT NEVER DEPRESSED

Up and down, down and up: business in the boom-and-bust climate of early BC (not to mention present-day BC) was never easy. As prospectors flooded into a town, businessmen and women followed, and the usual plethora of hotels, bars and brothels opened for business. As mines closed and miners fled for yet another El Dorado, businesses closed and their owners followed the prospectors out of town.

Even more solid communities had their failures, especially when BC was hit with one of its periodic depressions. One businessman in Chilliwack, battling the 1912 downturn, was ever optimistic, despite the unspecified oppressors who had beaten him down. The Chilliwack *Free Press* reported on July 25, 1912:

> Down and out, weakened but not broken. The hand of the oppressor has flattened me out, but I have sprouted up again. I am now holding forth at the Nevard Block where I hope to meet all my patrons and as many others as will favor me with a call. Although my business has been wrested from me I believe I still have the confidence and good will of the people of this place and that good will (with your permission) I wish to hand over to the new Company which is now forming and I hope you will patronize them as generously as you have me, and I believe you will find them worthy of the confidence with which I recommend them. The new firm is putting in a full line of furniture and house furnishings and promises to do wonders in the way of prices. Come and see them and don't forget I'll be there. Open Saturday, opposite Baptist church, temporary quarters.

Chapter Seven

Pigs, Potatoes and Pills for All Ills

PARANOMASIA

From the Victoria *Daily Colonist*, October 26, 1897:

The secretary of the Natural History Society begs to thank the officers and crew of the steamers Islander and Rainbow for their donation of $2.50 to the fund for the importation of British song birds to this province . . . This would seem to confirm the belief usually held that sailors are fond of a lark.

PATENTLY FALSE

Supplying liquor to Indians was a legal no-no for many years in British Columbia, but some accused came up with a novel defence. In 1894, a defendant on Cortes Island claimed he had supplied, not liquor, but a patent medicine called Burdock Blood Bitters.

The case was a tricky one. A woman named Kitty Coleman had gone to the logging camp where the unnamed defendant worked, and asked for whisky, of which there was none. The defendant said he would bring some whisky to Coleman's house as soon as he could get some, provided she would let a "half breed girl" of whom he was fond go away with him. But when the time came for him to collect his bride, he still had no liquor. Instead, he filled a whisky bottle with Burdock Blood Bitters and gave it to Coleman, saying "it was an extra good brand of whisky."

Coleman discovered the trick. Angered that she had not received the whisky she had been promised, she informed on the defendant. The Justice of the Peace wrote to the attorney general that BBB was, of course, on sale in almost every store and available to anyone who wanted to buy it. So, he asked, should the defendant be found guilty of supplying alcohol because he had pretended that BBB was whisky? There is no record of the response, but the joke was on the court: Burdock Blood Bitters, like many other patent medicines of the era developed in response to a strong temperance movement, was a so-called temperance drink, and contained twenty per cent alcohol.

PEEPING AT THOMAS

From the Victoria *Daily British Colonist*, October 4, 1860:

> Thos. E. Gray, a six-footer, and stout in proportion, complained before Judge Pemberton yesterday morning, of James S. Brown, a neighbor of his, who, he alleged had looked through his window and made threats against his person ... Gray ... said he could bring witnesses that Brown had threatened to maim him. Judge—Why do you suppose he is going to hurt you? Gray—For the simple reason that I believe him to be deranged ... Mr. Crease—Your honor, there has been nothing proved, except that my client looked through Gray's window; we admit that. Surely a "cat may look at a king." Judge—Certainly; but when that cat makes threats he must be looked after (laughter).

PERIPATETIC SPANIARDS

Petroglyphs etched in vermilion near Keremeos, hollowed-out tunnels in rock deep in the Vancouver Island rainforest: did Spaniards roam this region long before their documented visits?

Similkameen native legends and pictographs tell of a group of men with horses and helmets who entered their valley sometime in, perhaps, the 18th century. The men, presumed to be Spaniards who had come north from Mexico, fought with the Similkameen people, killed many, then retreated south. The next year they returned, but this time, the Similkameen killed them all. Their burial site is said to be at Spanish Mound, a still-undiscovered location northeast of Keremeos. And stories tell of artifacts such as leather helmets found somewhere near the town, though those artifacts have somehow been lost.

More dubious is the story of the lost mine—or lost monastery—of Leechtown, west of Victoria. In every version of the story—and there are many, some suggesting a mine manned by natives enslaved by the Spanish, others a monastery built by peripatetic Spanish monks—a lone man, prospector or hunter, is travelling through the forest when he comes upon a staircase hewn from the rock, almost hidden under moss and underbrush. He follows the stairs down to a tunnel and a gallery cut from the rock with hand chisels. In the gallery are, depending on the story, tools, weapons, artifacts, a long line of gold statues, a line of bullion ingots half a metre high and a metre deep, and/or skeletons in Spanish armour.

The man who finds this treasure promises to lead others to his find, but dies before he can do so. Or, he cannot find it again, or he decides it is better left alone. No one has ever been able to return to the site the lone traveller found, no matter how carefully he committed its location to memory.

PIG TALES

From the Pig War (see page 155) to pigs in the street, porcine antics were always good for a yarn. More often than not, the pigs outsmarted the people. From *BC 1887, A Ramble in British Columbia*:

> That gorgeously appointed and very comfortable and well-managed boat the *Olympian* landed us at Victoria early in the morning. Such a sight there was when a herd of pigs resplendent in colours which would make a rainbow feel dull were unshipped from somewhere below, and a clear road was made for them to rush past the custom-house officers, who wanted to count them. There was a brief pause, during which the verb Damn was conjugated with great rapidity in several keys. Then a bar was withdrawn, and a squealing, grunting, parti-coloured streak of swinery went scuttering past the bewildered officials, and was lost to sight in the street. One turned to the other and said
> "Seventy-two. What did you make them?"
> "Make them" was the wrathful retort; "who the blazes would make anything of such things as those? Enough to give one d.t."

From the same book:

> It appeared that quite recently a cargo of dynamite had mysteriously disappeared, and after diligent but fruitless search it had been decided that "those blamed pigs

had eaten it," and consequently the following notice was posted up on the walls of the more important buildings in the city (i.e. the Queen's Hotel and another shack):

"Notice is hereby given that the Pigs of Golden City have consumed 40 lbs. or more of dynamite. Parties are therefore requested to refrain from pricking or otherwise abusing them on pain of an explosion."

"By Order of the Mayor."

The *Kootenay Mail* in Revelstoke took up the theme on June 18, 1894:

Those people who keep pigs should also keep the law, and confine their porkers in their own domains. My neighbor's chickens delight in scratching my garden and destroy quite a lot of flowers, but when my neighbor's pig puts his massive head under my gate and lifts it off its hinges I think it time to protest. I hope the constable will at once see that those people confine their pigs within limits. It will be too late after a garden has been despoiled and a dead pig lying in the middle of it.

Indeed, piggy depredations might call for very serious measures. In

1872, someone in the Department of Lands and Water wrote to the attorney general, protesting about pigs. "The hogs are rooting in Humboldt St. [Victoria]," he complained, "and really damaging the backing of the road. In Saanich, Comox, & other Country Districts, they have done and are constantly doing pest damages to the Roads, especially to those newly made." The writer called upon the attorney general to enforce the Swine Act.[1]

PIG WAR

The First World War was triggered by the shooting of a nobleman; BC's only war was triggered by the shooting of a pig. In 1859, after the rest of the border between BC and the United States had been settled by treaty, Britain and the US were still debating over which country owned the San Juan Islands. One day, a large black pig owned by the Hudson's Bay Company on San Juan Island, wandered into the yard of Lyman Cutlar, an American farmer. Cutler shot the pig; HBC farm manager Charles Griffin demanded $100 compensation. Cutler offered $10; Griffin refused. Maybe Cutlar said the pig was eating his potatoes and maybe Griffin replied, "It is up to you to keep your potatoes out of my pig," or maybe not.

The British said they would arrest Cutlar; Cutlar demanded protection from American troops—and the Pig War was on. Soon there were warships standing offshore and troops standing on the land, and insults flying between the two sides—though no bullets. Then the troops were stood down and a joint occupation agreed on: thus, American Camp and English Camp, which still exist as parks on San Juan Island today. After twelve years, an arbitration committee gave the San Juans to the United States. Justifiably angered that Britain had not stood up to the Americans, Canadians—for by then, BC had joined Canada—lobbied for more control over their own foreign affairs.

PILLS FOR ALL ILLS

Throughout North America, makers of patent medicines placed ads in every magazine and newspaper, promising instant relief from whatever ailed you. Scrofula or King's Evil, boils or tumours, salt rheum, ringworm, syphilis, neuralgia, fever, dumb ague and jaundice, plus a whole horde of other sufferings, could be cured with this tonic or those pills. "Thin girls get plump while using Dr. A.W. Chase's nerve tonic," trumpeted the Rossland *Miner* in August of 1899. And Rossland men weak, broken, or discouraged from effects of excesses, worry, and overwork, could be cured by just sending money to the Erie Medical Company who would dispatch the appropriate appliances and remedies. Or Rosslandites could travel down to Spokane to be cured by Dr. Reeves, who had, declared the testimonials, cured this person or that of deafness, eye pain and blurring of vision, stomach (belching, bloating and sour risings), consumption (tuberculosis), heart disease, catarrh, liver troubles, asthma, and, presumably, every and any other ailment. He could even cure a weak back, which, left untreated, would bring "an untimely death."

Meanwhile, sufferers in any town or backwoods of BC could buy in a store or order by mail such marvellous cures as Sarsaparilla, sugar-coated pills that were *the* great cure, stomach bitters, or a huge number of other preparations. And Victoria men could take heart: if they would just travel to Seattle to meet with Dr. Ratcliffe, they could be cured of "lost manhood, vital losses, exhausting drains, impotency and all sexual disorders of young, middle-aged and old men."

PLUM TASTY

From the Atlin *Claim*, December 9, 1899:

> Talk about hard times! Why, we could tell our readers of a certain unpretentious little shack not "steen" blocks from Discovery street, where no less than five whole plum puddings are dangling in all their saccherine glory from the ridge pole. We think it would be unwise to designate the locality more clearly until we have had a chance at them ourselves.

POLICE AND RAIDING RESULTS

Gambling dens and illicit drink and opium parlours existed in almost every town in BC. From time to time, often prompted by outraged newspaper editorials, various authorities decided to cleanse their towns—and that often meant cleansing the police department. In Prince George at the end of the First World War, police commissioners determined on a "complete cleanup in the city police department," and began by suspending the chief. At the end of their meeting, before word of the crackdown could leak out, they sent a raiding squad to one of the "gambling dives and Chinese premises." There, they found opium paraphernalia and a "seemingly well equipped 'hop joint.'" Everyone on the scene was arrested.

Following one of the Chinese men who escaped, a policeman "was led into a neighboring shack, where a full-sized game of draw in which several white men were participating, was discovered."[2] Everyone was arrested, tried, convicted and fined.

The commissioners, said the paper, were being congratulated on their firm stand, and lawlessness in Prince George was in retreat.

There was more to come. A month later, 21 Chinese were arrested for gambling and convicted. Twenty accepted a prison term, and ended up cutting wood in the forest for 30 days; one agreed to pay a fine. "The exception is believed to be the winner of the jackpot finished just before the police squad arrived."

Then the reason for the police commission's actions became a little clearer. Reported the Prince George paper, "A mystery, dark and deep, pervades the atmosphere in the region of the city hall. The mystery is attached to the disappearance of 52 quarts of whisky and seven full-grown cans of opium. This aggregation of undiluted joy was obtained by police in a raid on Chinese quarters last August and was ordered confiscated by the magistrate. Until the last few days it was supposed to still be in the custody of the police, but a search has failed to reveal even the aroma of the missing stuff.

"Last night the commissioners decided to inform the attorney-general's department of the strange disappearance and request his advice on the procedure to be taken in a further search."[3]

In Rossland in 1899, the police commissioners heard charges that various policemen had taken bribes to overlook Chinese gambling houses. The public rushed in to the hearings, laughing and joking throughout. Li Hong, a Chinatown merchant, testified he collected $12 from each of five gambling houses, and took the money to an official at the jail. "The Chinaman believed that if money was not paid every month the houses in which gambling was carried on would be raided." By May, the amount was $15 per house. In June, the jail official said that wasn't enough.

Not only gamblers were required to pay off the police, according to witnesses. A woman named Annie Maloney said police asked her for $20 when she arrived in town. "She informed the official she was only in the city on a visit and did not pay them any money."[4] And on the hearing went, with witness after witness testifying to the bribery fund.

POTATOES

From the potato king of Ladner to the potatoes to be exhibited at the 1911 World's Fair in New York, spuds were often in the Fraser Valley news. And sometimes, they were cause for potato tales, as in a story that made the front page of the Chilliwack *Free Press* on September 28, 1911:

> A peculiar experience was the lot of Chas. Parker, the Clothier, the other day. He went into his garden to raise

some potatoes, when a large one stubbornly adhered to mother earth, and in an effort to raise it by hand, he raised the nail off the third finger of the left hand. This is a true potato story and a very sore finger is now a constant reminder to Mr. Parker that when he again desires to raises Chilliwack Valley potatoes, he had better use a small block and tackle, or at least a good spade.

PROSPECTOR'S PARABLE

The Zeballos *Miner* ran this tale on June 13, 1938, copied from a board nailed to a placer lease on the shores of Nootka Sound:

He that sitteth upon a hot stove shall arise there-of. Yea, I say unto you go thou to the right 660 ft. and at right angles turn left and walk 660 feet. And upon that spot place a post marked Final and affixing thereto a legal tag No. 396485. There upon continue on the same line yet another 660 ft. turn yet again at right angles to the left and walk 2640 ft. turning to the left at right angles and measure 110 staff lengths and upon that spot place a post; mark ye this post Initial; and affix thereto the counterpart of the legal tag 396485 also upon this post mark ye well with indelible pencil claiming all within these boundaries. Rim to rim of river sediment only. Cherish this ground until the time be ripe for there cometh a miracle and the land may be rich in specks of gold, 950 fine; then dig ye well even unto the bedrock and wash that which thou hast dug, mostly clay and muck and many other things which have been placed in thy claim. Cometh yet another miracle and thou hast found many colors in thy cleanup box—yea, those fine colors shall make thee rich and thy wife shall be richer and thy daughters shall have many fine suitors who shall not be rich; make them thy servants to dig muck on thy claim and when thou art absent they also will become rich, even beyond thy understanding, thou wilt shake thy head and mutter, 'what the hell!' and many other oaths shall escape from thy mouth; then thou must stake thee another claim for the many fine colors will have vanished.

RABID ROBBERS

Though crime occurred all across North America, and bank robberies were fairly frequent, some of BC's robberies were unusual enough to make the big American newspapers. This account appeared in the *New York Times* on January 27, 1912:

Two masked men entered the Hill Crest Branch of the Royal Bank of Canada, at Main Street and Seventeenth Avenue [Vancouver], in broad daylight to-day, drove Mr. Steaves, the manager and one of his clerks into the vault, knocked the other clerk unconscious with a blow from a revolver, and escaped with $1,999, all the money in the till.

According to one of the bank officials, the first man to enter the bank pointed his revolver at Manager Steaves, while the other man covered Harrison, the ledger keeper, and Richmond, the teller, ordering them to hold up their hands.

Harrison and Richmond were some distance from the thief, and the latter, instead of complying at once with the command, backed out of his cage quickly and threw the keys into a box inside, at the same time slamming the cage door. As he stepped out the door locked itself with the keys inside, a manoeuvre which compelled the robbers to hunt for a poker, which they used to reach through for the keys. The bandits ordered their prisoners to enter the vault. Harrison demurred, upon which one of the men said to his companions:

"Let's shoot him."

"No, I'll shoot him," said the other, and felled Harrison.

The police have a good description of the men, but have no idea of the direction they took in escaping.

RAIN

From the Zeballos *Miner*, May 30, 1938:

Newspaper and magazine stories have broadcast widely our energetic rains. So much so that even tourists now arrive with hip boots. For the information of the outside we must add that it does not rain here all the time. We have actually had brisk dust storms during the past few days.

RIDING RECORD

Horses and riding were a big part of early BC, mostly taken for granted as the mainstay of early transportation. Occasionally, though, a horse ride through the wilderness was worthy of comment.

One such was the record ride undertaken by Mexican Tom guiding J.S. Cowper between Queen Charlotte City and Massett. Though the 120-mile (195-kilometre) trip was considered a three-day ride, the two men galloped—through a blinding storm for much of the way—in twenty-three hours, trying to catch the steamer *Prince John* at Massett.

They rode seven and a half hours to a ranch on the Tlell River, rested a few hours, then carried on to Mexican Tom's place, where they rested again to wait until tidal rivers en route could be forded. Drenched to the skin, trusting to the horses to find the trail in pitch darkness, they arrived at Massett at 11:15 PM "The feature of the ride was the splendid performance of the Mexican's young mare Annie Laurie, which carried Mr. Cowper the entire journey," reported the Queen Charlotte *Islander*, "wearing out two relays of older horses, and finishing the trying journey in a fresh condition. She has never been broken to the saddle and it was not expected at the start that she could last more than half the journey, but she covered the long journey ... in the teeth of a gale, without whip or spur, finding her way in and out and over the drift logs on the eastern shore of Graham Island in the darkness."[5]

The men reached the dock in time. The steamer, however, was late.

A ROGUE AND A VAGABOND

A rogue and a vagabond sounds like a fine romantic notion: the wandering trickster who might scam or hoax you, the sunny-mooded man—and almost always a male—with a knapsack on his back and no more than a penny in his pocket. But from Tudor times in England, the rogue and vagabond was taken seriously indeed: a dangerous man whose actions, or even just existence, threatened the proper order of society. Found guilty of this catch-all crime, which could include anything from running scams to begging to being a nuisance on the streets, he could be punished by being severely whipped and branded on the right ear, thus carrying forever the mark of his transgressions.

The crime continues to exist in various parts of the world, from Britain to Mauritius to the Bahamas to the state of Maryland. Not that long ago in Britain, the courts declared an offender a rogue and a vagabond, and imposed a fine of £100 for this second offence, with a warning that if the man was found guilty a third time, the penalty would be much more severe.

Inheriting the British legal system, colonial and early provincial BC declared it a crime to be a rogue and a vagabond. But, befitting a society on the edge of nowhere, where a man might often find himself wandering from place to place without any money, BC often gave the accused the benefit of the doubt, provided that he left town on the next steamer. Sometimes, though, an accused tried the patience of the courts severely, and was treated severely in return. The Victoria *Daily British Colonist* reported on January 12, 1870:

> A man giving the name of John Welch, who leaned on a crutch and wore a moustache of formidable dimensions, was brought before Mr. Pemberton yesterday on a charge of being a rogue and a vagabond. He said he had lost his feet and was waiting for a steamer to come and take him to San Francisco ... He was an Englishman, had fought in four wars, and had gone two days in Victoria without eating a bite. The Inspector of Police said that the man had got an order to go to the hospital, and made a great row there disturbing the patients. 'Here,' said the Inspector, 'are two pistols he's been in the habit of flourishing around the saloons, threatening to shoot people.' The prisoner, who talked incessantly, said that he had come from White Pine, where a man had to carry pistols to protect himself from the Indians. He was remanded for three days.

John Rooney was also charged with being a rogue and a vagabond. He did not go down quietly. From the Victoria *Daily British Colonist* on September 25, 1863:

> Prisoner—How am I a rogue? What have I done?
> Sergeant Blake—You have gone into Indian houses and taken things against their will.
> Rooney—I say I did not; they gave them to me.
> Mr. Ehrenbacker was then called, who stated that prisoner had been in his shop helping himself to fruit, and when

ordered out he commenced to be abusive, and threw apples about.

Rooney—You're a liar, sir, and the truth is not in you. (Laughter.)

Mr. Pemberton (to prisoner)—Mind what you are about; you are in the hands of justice.

Rooney—Oh, there's no justice in this court. (Laughter)

[Rooney] To witness—Did you kick me?

Witness—I did not kick you.

Rooney—You did, you vagabond. Tell the truth: you kicked me and threw apples at me. (Laughter.) . . .

[Pemberton convicted Rooney of being a rogue and a vagabond, and sentenced him to three months at hard labour.]

Rooney—I don't care a cent for your hard labor. (Laughter.)

Mr. Pemberton—Perhaps that will put you in your senses.

Rooney—I am in my senses and I'll put you in yours before I've done with you. (Laughter.)

In an 1866 case, Sam Williams was found guilty as charged and sentenced to three months on the chain gang. He was, said the paper, quite indifferent about being called a rogue, but much incensed at being branded a vagabond.

ROLLING ALONG

Roller skates were invented in the 18th century, but it was only in the 1860s that someone developed easily usable four-wheel skates. Roller skating became a popular pastime around 1900 and roller rinks opened around BC. But it wasn't roller derby; a more genteel sport was described in the Chilliwack *Free Press*, October 12, 1911:

The Free Press man casually stepped into the Roller rink last Friday night. That Chilliwack has a first class roller rink conducted on lines strictly adhering to cleanliness, healthful recreation, gentlemanly and womanly deportment, attention and courtesy is at once apparent . . . The skating space is about ninety feet long, well lighted and floored with two-inch maple. Two hundred pairs of roller skates are ready for service. A $1600 sixteen piece band instrument, the latest, and best of its kind in the province, driven by electric or water power, with a selection of fifty different pieces of music, furnishes the tuneful melodies, to which the young people glide, in graceful fashion. Smoking is prohibited and any divergence from the rules of good conduct is speedily dealt with.

Chapter Eight
Sea Serpents, Suicides and Theatre in the Wilds

SAFE NOT SAFE

If there is treasure, thieves will follow, and where there are safes, there are safecrackers. On June 1, 1907, the Port Essington *Sun* reported:

The north coast is taking on the mantle of up-to-date civilization.

The man with the jimmy, mask and powder has arrived and made his debut here last night in the ancient and peaceful village of [Port] Simpson.

The Hudson's Bay Co.'s safe was dynamited in attempted burglary. The office door was broken and the combination in the safe pried off with tools taken from the store. Socks, sugar and blankets were piled around the safe to deaden the report. All the joints were filled with soap. The burglar was evidently disturbed in his work by the entrance of the steamer *Henrietta* at 3 in the morning and hurriedly retreated.

Next morning it was found that the safe was charged with nitroglycerine, which the manager, Mr. Sharp, had set off to get at the contents.

The bottom of the safe was blown out . . . The burglar was rewarded with $25 taken from a small basket in the office.

Safecrackers tried to blow up a safe at the butcher's shop in Chilliwack in 1912. They broke in through a rear door and placed their nitroglycerine. But they used so much explosive that the safe was blown to pieces and the front window smashed to smithereens. A patrolling policeman heard the bang and hurried to the scene in time to see three men running away. The thieves got $80 in cash, $70 in cheques and presumably some dented eardrums. They left behind a carpenter's chisel.

The following morning, the same men attempted to blow up a safe in Cloverdale. The noise brought people to the store before the men could get anything—though, again, they left behind a carpenter's chisel.

SEA SERPENTS

In the lake or in the sea, serpent-like creatures whose bodies extended ten or twenty metres and undulated sinuously below, then above, the water's surface, appeared regularly to credulous onlookers. Victoria's Cadborosaurus and the Okanagan's Ogopogo have garnered most of the publicity, but they were far from alone. And never, never, never, could the envisioned monstrous serpent be a whale or porpoise, seen through a glass darkly, or simply glimpsed in the gloaming by a half-asleep mariner. No, each of these beasts was real and terrifying—especially when reported in the paper.

Take a Mr. Stewart, for example, who told his story to the Vancouver *News Advertiser* in July of 1890. He and some fellow loggers had been crossing Howe Sound in a boat when they saw a strange black log, straight as an arrow and about twenty-five metres long. But when they headed towards it, it sank "like a stone"; the boaters were "deeply astonished" and, despite the fear that the log would surface under their boat and overturn them, they waited for it to show itself again. Nothing happened, so they headed for home once more. And, behold, the log reappeared now on their left and closer. It sank, reappeared, and blew a stream of water at them, drenching every man. As it began lashing the water with its tail, the men were convinced: this was a sea serpent. Off they rowed as fast as they could, with the beast in hot pursuit. Fortunately, the animal desisted and the men reached shore safely. They swore the beast was not a whale, but refused to declare it a sea serpent, just saying it was "an inhabitant of the sea not very often met with."[1]

In 1933, the Vancouver *Province* ran a letter from a Nakusp man, who reported with great precision that, while steaming at an even seven knots north-north-east up the Upper Arrow Lake at 11:32 AM, on November 14, he had sighted the head of a sea serpent over the port bow. He set course for the beast, and seven minutes later, the head "was about 6-yards abeam . . . We dare not go closer as the bow-wave from the sea serpent's prow would have swamped my 90-foot cruiser. Continuing on our course we passed the tail at 11.48. My crew guessed the speed of the reptile at four knots."

The 1930s may have been a bad time for the economy, but they were a good time for reports of sea monsters and other strange occurrences. In 1934, articles ran in newspapers across the continent, including the *New York Times*, reporting a strange, reddish-coloured sea monster found dead on a beach by a Prince Rupert fisherman, a serpent ten metres long, with skin like sandpaper, partly covered by hair and partly by spines or quills, with a head like that of a horse. Many spectators had their pictures taken behind the long, scrawny creature and people were quick to recall that three such unidentified creatures had been reported along the Pacific coast in the previous two years. But the story barely had time to take hold of the public imagination before it was debunked. Though a director of the Dominion fisheries experimental station expressed himself as puzzled by the beast, and declared the reddish flesh suggested it was a mammal, not a reptile, a spoil-sport biologist soon determined that it was simply a two-months-dead and somewhat decayed basking shark.

SHOCKED AND APPALLED

From the Atlin *Claim*, May 17, 1899:

> We claim to have some little morality and common decency and object to having our feelings perpetually shocked by loud mouthed voicings of the most filthy obscenity and hair-raising blasphemy. Every evening the late outspewings from the barrooms flock down here prepared for any deviltry. More liquor is easily obtained in the brothels and the result is pandemonium. We claim the protection against these crying evils to which we are legally entitled, and hope to get it before half of us are dead from insomnia or are driven into madness.

The letter writer apparently got his wish. Even before the letter was published, the authorities stepped in and fined the evildoers $30 each.

SHOT, NOT QUITE BY A STRANGER

From the Revelstoke *Kootenay Mail*, April 14, 1894:

William Boyd, who keeps the 70-Mile House, Cariboo road was accidentally shot on the 20th inst. While returning home from Clinton he passed a stranger and offered to take his overcoat on with him so as to ease the stranger's load. When Boyd got home and took the things out of the rig, he threw the overcoat and other articles on the floor, when a pistol went off. The bullet entered Boyd's side above the hip, circled around the body and now lies buried in the shoulder. The doctor says that no vital part has been touched and unless blood poisoning sets in, there will not be much danger. Mr. Boyd is well known amongst old timers here and is a very popular host. He is rapidly recovering.

SIDEWALK ATTACKS

Town drunks and infant towns and cities with little money for building sidewalks and roads were rarely a good combination. The Victoria *British Colonist* noted on July 13, 1859:

J.C. Graham was lifted into court this morning by the police. One side of his face was much bruised and his legs so shattered that he was unable to use them. He had fallen off the sidewalk whilst intoxicated at the south end of Government street, late on Sunday evening, and was picked up and conveyed to the Police Office. He was discharged.

SIGHTSEEING

From the Bella Coola *Courier*, September 28, 1912:

A party of Ocean Falls ladies took a spin down the Inlet one sunny afternoon this week... [They] stated that they saw a school of whales, one bear (on the beach) and several goats on the mountain side; but it was not much of an afternoon for sightseeing. They expect to do better the next trip.

SKUNK CABBAGE

Slow news days and half-empty columns in small-town newspapers called forth many an editor's creative juices. But it must have been a slow news day indeed, and a twisted sense of humour, that prompted editor "Mack," tongue firmly inserted in cheek, to invite housewives to use skunk cabbage as a salad vegetable, for skunk cabbage leaves are poisonous. They also contain needle-like crystals of calcium oxalate, which can really hurt—and may cause swelling unto death. There were no reports, however, of such a result; perhaps Prince Rupert women were too sensible to take this heavy-handed humour seriously. From the Prince Rupert *Daily News*, May 1, 1911:

Young housewives just starting out to make hubbies happy in Prince Rupert will hail with joy the ubiquitous appearance throughout the muskeg of the succulent Skunk Cabbage. The beautiful golden hued frondage of this delightful herb upspringing all over the townsite gladdens the eye giving us assurance that Spring is here. Few varieties of esculenta possess stronger claims to the attention of the epicure or make their presence felt more effectively in their season. At a time of year when the humble Seattle cabbage is perhaps less attractive to the shopper than it might be comes the Skunk Cabbage redolent with all the fresh fragrance for which it is famous.

Unrivalled as a salad vegetable, the Skunk Cabbage may also be boiled, fried, stewed, toasted, grilled, steamed or baked. Its attractions as a table delicacy remain equally powerful no matter what way of cooking may be adopted. This aromatic vegetable possesses a particular charm for the young housewife, as it is absolutely proof against even the most experienced culinary attacks, and preserves its own peculiar delicacy of flavor even if left on the stove till there is barely a cinder of its fragrant foliage left. Played up as a little surprise upon the young husband it is an unfailing source of domestic felicity. Its presence in the home is an influence that lingers.

Just one hint to the young bride anxious to try this novel Spring delicacy; in gathering the Skunk Cabbage use a sharp very long-handled knife, wear a thick pair of impervious gloves and a respirator. It is always advisable to keep to windward of the vegetable while cutting it.

SLOT MACHINES, BEATING

Rare is the player who consistently wins at the slot machines by feeding in coin after coin, especially at early machines that could easily be tilted in favour of the owner. So some tried other methods. In 1919, a burglar forced his way into a Prince George poolroom late at night, carried out a slot machine and beat it to pieces with an axe. "He evidently discovered by practical experience that this was the only sure method of beating a slot machine."

The burglar had entered various Prince George premises over the previous two weeks. An accomplice and a small white dog were also members of the gang. "In the opinion of one local Sherlock the desperadoes will now proceed to camouflage the dog with a coat of yellow paint," wagged the Prince George *News*.[2]

SMUGGLERS

Whisky and rum, clothing and guns: if you could hide it, you could smuggle it between British Columbia and the United States. Nineteenth-century women had an advantage in the smuggling game, since their clothes were often voluminous and a male detective would be greeted with shrieks of outrage should he attempt to investigate a crinoline or hoop skirt. But, in December of 1870, the US customs department appointed a female inspector—who later came to a bad end (see *Suicide, Mrs. Hurd*, page 182)—who was to travel on the Puget Sound steamers and watch for contraband. Less than a month later, the number of women on board had decreased to almost none. An American paper attributed this to the presence of the inspector, but the Victoria *Daily Colonist* disagreed, claiming that the fact that it was Christmastime probably had more to do with the decrease. But one could well understand, said the editorialist, if American women flocked to Victoria, for the town boasted a "splendid array of rich and fashionable French and English goods at prices which are in such astounding contrast with those on the other side [that they] must be quite irresistible to the ladies of Puget Sound"—if true, it is the first recorded BC instance of cross-border shopping.[3]

SNOWMOBILES, AN EARLY VERSION

Those who find fault with the roar and thunder of snowmobiles racing across the land would have approved of an earlier version operating in the northern town of Stewart in the winter of 1927. The vehicle got good reviews for its speed, compared to that of horse-drawn vehicles, in the Portland Canal *News* on December 30, 1927:

In appearance it resembles a small caterpillar tractor, having the typical travelling steel belt link for bearing surface. This belt is fitted onto the ordinary rear wheels of a Ford car, and an extra pair of wheels in front of those. Instead of front wheels, runners are substituted, five feet long and eight inches wide. This machine steers like an ordinary car, and develops a speed of 20 miles an hour under favorable conditions . . . This winter's snow (12 feet to date) is such as to give any vehicle a severe test, and if the Snowmobile continues to stand up to its present performance it may simplify the problem of winter transportation in this district.

SPIRITUALISM

Can you find gold by appealing to the spirits? Certainly, declared a Mrs. Semon, who, with her husband, prospected on Lorne Creek, a tributary of the Skeena River. According to someone they hired, the workmen would get their picks and shovels ready each morning, then wait for Mrs. Semon to emerge from her tent, where she was having breakfast. She would put on a blindfold, and take up a wand, then stand up arrow straight, snap her fingers and hum a tune. As her husband led her along a gravel bar, she would stop and jab the wand into the gravel, shouting, "Here is the gold!" The men would then dig deep, but never with any result. After a summer of shouting and digging, the Semons and their spirits headed back south to California.[4]

Spiritualism was a popular belief, but one spiritualist who performed in Victoria in December of 1894 stubbed his theatrical toe. Twenty-six people paid 50 cents each to see his performance. He declared that he had married a beautiful young lady but she got tired of seeing him in two places, astral and physical, at once, and went back to her family. No wonder, shouted an audience member: seeing him in one place would be quite enough.

The evening did not improve. At the end of the performance, all twenty-six demanded, and received, their money back.

SUICIDE

Depression is no modern ailment. Men and women far from home, with no money and no hope, or ill with serious diseases, or made crazy by their inescapable circumstances, or just down and depressed, found a remarkable variety of ways to commit suicide.

Mrs. Freeman, the ex-wife of a man who committed suicide at Pine City, near Atlin, in April of 1899, was outraged that newspaper reports said that Mr. Freeman was living with her. "He was not. I have been living alone ever since we mutually agreed to separate three years ago. We separated at Skaguay. We couldn't get along together. He went south to California and I came to the Summit . . ." The first she saw of Freeman was when she met him unexpectedly near town. "For the nonce I forgot myself and spoke first. He spoke also. We both conversed and then he asked me to sit down on the edge of the road and talk over old times. I told he was not a fit man for any woman to sit down with on a road's edge."

The two went back to Atlin, where Mrs. Freeman left her ex-husband. But he chased her down in Pine City and asked to enter her tent. She refused. "He went away and in about an hour he returned. This time he did not wait for an invitation. He stepped in and as he did he said: 'So you won't let me in eh' well, it's all off, and as he said this he pulled a gun out of his pocket, placed it over his left nipple and fell backward, dead."[5]

Many others also opted for suicide. The Zeballos *Miner* reported on July 11, 1938:

> A man at Kalskino Inlet a few days ago blew himself up with dynamite ... It is believed the suicide sat on a box of dynamite and touched it off ... The suicide was blown to pieces, his head and shoulders being found in a tree.

The Prince Rupert *Sun* noted another case on June 29, 1907:

> J. Robertson, a prospector, in the vicinity of Hazelton, is reported to have committed suicide in the Driftwood because he could not buy a bottle of whisky for $20.

The Revelstoke *Kootenay Mail* ran a letter on April 14, 1894:

> When Mr. Jowson said he thought Mason had a decent funeral last May, I thought I would like to ask him to define his ideas of decency. Putting aside the unearthly hour at which the funeral was appointed—7 o'clock in the morning—putting aside the fact that none of the deceased friends were notified of the time for starting; allowing that $20 was quite enough to spend on the

funeral of a supposed suicide (although he left a watch and chain worth $150, besides a new overcoat and other things); also putting aside the fact that the body was carted away unwashed, even with the boots left on; allowing all these things to pass, I would like to ask Mr. Howson if he thought it was decent to put the corpse into the ground and shovel in the earth and stones without the reading of some kind of service at the graveside? It has always been the custom in Christian countries to read the burial service before the grave is filled in, unless the deceased person is a suicide, and in Mr. Mason's case, it was never proved that he took his life wilfully. That he took an overdose to procure sleep is the general belief of all who knew him.

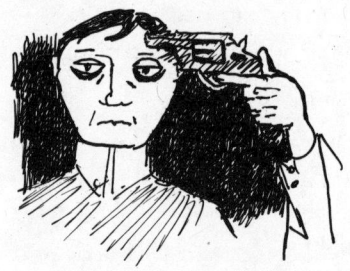

From the Victoria *Daily British Colonist*, September 13, 1884:

A sickening suicide is reported from the Washington Territory asylum of the insane. Mrs. Anna Jacobs, better known along the Sound and here as Mrs. Jared Hurd, a patient under treatment, eluded the attention of her attendants, and entered the bathroom. She was a large, powerful woman, and being violently insane, was kept in a straight jacket to prevent her doing injury to herself and others. This, however, did not prevent her from turning on the hot-water faucet with her teeth. Lying down in the tub she placed herself directly below the scalding stream and allowed it to run into her mouth. When her absence was discovered search was made, and she was found in the bathtub dead, and her flesh cooked!

... Her end under such shocking circumstances will strike her former friends with a thrill of horror.

From the Phoenix *Pioneer*, January 21, 1911:

After cutting his throat from ear to ear, a man by the name of Lester in one of the K.V. construction camps near Merritt, plunged into a river and completed his voyage into the hereafter.

A telegram was sent from Sicamous to the attorney general, January 27, 1892:

Dewdney shot himself last night about six PM. Made enquiries and a letter he wrote states that he might as well take his life as die in an asylum.

The Victoria *British Colonist* reported a sad case from New Westminster on November 4, 1859:

On Friday last ... news arrived that Mrs. Crote, the wife of one of the Sappers and Miners, had murdered her family and cut her own throat ... By the evidence before the coroner's inquest that was summoned the same day, it appeared that she had been in a desponding way for some time about being out here . . .

Mrs. Crote had apparently been greatly disturbed by the murder of three men by local Indians, and had said that "sooner than the Indians should kill her children she would kill them herself." After a restless night, she did so, taking the lives of her eight-year-old son, three-year-old daughter, her baby and herself, all with a straight razor.

Occasionally, a person bent on self-destruction posed a difficult dilemma for friends or officials in the neighbourhood. In April 1880, Justice of the Peace and government agent Henry Fry wrote to the attorney general from Maple Bay on Vancouver Island. He needed, he said, some advice at once. "A French Settler by the name of Francis Deucide has a Mania that his time is come and that he's going to die, has given away all his effects even to his cooking utensils, Bed, bedding and Clothes, has taken no food for several days and cannot be persuaded to do so."

Fry visited Deucide and found him rational, but completely disinclined to change his mind. "He replied in perfect good humour and with the politeness of his nation that as he owed no man a cent and the things were his own he thought he was a free agent and had a right to do as he liked." Fry appealed to a Catholic priest and an Anglican reverend for help, but neither could sway the man from his chosen course. "But the man must be out of his mind to do what he has done. He wrote out a Paper in French which I have seen and in which he gives to two of his neighbors all his Personal Effects consisting of Cattle, Hay, Grain, . . . Furniture Cooking Utensils and all the Food in the House to each an equal moiety and the worst of it is that they have taken them all away and left the man with bare Walls."

Deucide was determined to starve himself to death. "Can I

won ... Kid Gallagher got a decision and the prize money over D. Kelly in a three-round bout ... The wrestling match advertised did not come off.

THANKS, BUT NO THANKS

Not everyone thought BC was the promised land—at least, not a land that fulfilled its promises. Good thing writer Stephen Redgrave, a returning officer in the Kootenay in 1890, can't see the difference between BC and Saskatchewan land prices now. He wrote in the Toronto *Globe and Mail* on January 18, 1868:

> I would sooner have a mile square in the Saskatchewan valley, than all British Columbia, and would be thankful to get out of such a miserable, wretched place. I should advise the Canadian government to have nothing to do with a country which can neither support a bank, build a church, or obtain £20,000 as a loan, to save it from general bankruptcy. I should like to give your correspondent a description of British Columbia; but my space will not permit me; I must therefore dismiss the subject for the present.

THAT'S DYNAMITE

Building the Grand Trunk Pacific east from the infant city of Prince Rupert between 1908 and 1911 was not a simple task: rocks to blast, grades to surmount, muskeg to conquer. Most of the work took a healthy helping of dynamite, but in a "city" where shacks were more common than sturdy buildings, where to store the explosives? Some bright boy decided the local blacksmith's shop would be a fine place to legally send him ... as a lunatic for Medical examination and pay the expenses?" inquired Fry.

The reply, if any was sent, came too late: Francis Deucide died on May 9 of voluntary starvation.[6]

SURPRISE AMUSEMENTS

Residents of Surprise, near Atlin in northwest BC, celebrated the Queen's birthday with a variety of amusements. From the Atlin *Claim*, May 17, 1899:

The day's program started out with pistols and ended with a concert in the evening, and the choicest viand on bill of fare was this here concert. The music of Surprise is good, and doubly so when you find that one guitar in the company is made from a Sunlight soap box ... N. Caspinson, a trick violinist, offered more sport, in imitating a preacher preaching, a donkey braying and a barber cutting hair with bones ... Another very unusual contest and seeming out of place was the ugly face competition. Mrs. Caspinson won this hands down ... The ham on the greasy pole was won by W. Hunt of the Stickine ... In the cockfight, D. Kelly put 75 sticks with caps attached. No problem: life went on as usual for several weeks, until a spark flew from the anvil to the storage box. The blacksmith noticed and ran for cover—just in time, as the dynamite exploded and the blacksmith's shop flew into the air in small pieces. The explosion shattered every window in the neighbouring Central Hotel, among the thousand windows broken by the explosion. And one guest had a rude awakening when he was hurled out of bed and hit the floor head first.[7]

THAT'S FER DAMSHUR

Of all the newspaper editors in all of the small towns in BC, Margaret Lally "Ma" Murray was the best-known and the longest lived; she vied for the title of most outrageous with pioneer editor Robert Lowery (see *Lowery of the* Ledge, page 117). She ran her newspaper in Bridge River-Lillooet through the Depression and on past the Second World War. During the war, sensing a new opportunity in the north as workers poured in to build the Alaska Highway, she started the *Alaska Highway News* in Fort St. John. Profiled in *Maclean's* magazine in 1966 as the salty sage of the Alaska Highway, she continued writing and kicking butt well into her seventies. Though her editorials, which often closed with "And that's fer damshur!," became her trademark, the news columns of her papers also overflowed with colourful language, mixed metaphors and mangled grammar. She waxed eloquent in the *Alaska Highway News* on June 28, 1945:

> It has taken only one generation to polish off the habit of women wearing corsets. For two generations we have been calling them foundation garments. Since the days of ancient Rome up to the 20th century women found it expedient to hold themselves together in corsets. Physicians, for lack of a better target, blamed many of women's ills on to wearing the corset. Pre-War One had the stays on the run. Post-War One saw them almost extinct. From the way women are now losing out—divorces, cancer, etc.; the alarming rate of deaths due to heart conditions—proves that the women are not much better off without corsets. A crusade for women to "hold themselves in"—in more ways than stays—is now due!

She wrote vividly in the Bridge River-Lillooet *News* on June 14, 1934:

> Last week on the Bridge River road one of the big Hayes Anderson trucks owned by the Evans Transportation, slid

off the bank of the bridge, turned over twice and dived into the muddy slime of the river.

The driver was knocked unconscious and smashed up. The truck! How could it help being smashed? It settled comfortably into the mud until the great cables dragged it up the bank. Sitting in the middle of the road its wheels on terra firma again, Curley stepped on the gas, it heaved and coughed, mud dripped from its innards and water flew from the chassis, he put the clutch in low and released her, and she clumsily started out, and came into Shalalth over the mountain on her own steam. "All in a day," stated Curley.

She promised a chuckle once a week and a belly laugh once a month. Perhaps her most famous editorial, one that got her into *Time* magazine, admonished the people of Fort St. John to conserve water. "There has been a terrible waste of water in this small town," she wrote. "We get our water the hard way, via a pipeline. We sure as hell need to use less if we are going to have this modern convenience, to head off this catastrophe, only flush for no. 2, curtail bathing to the Saturday night tub, go back to the old washrag, which could always move a lot of B.O. if applied often enough."[8] People laughed, but Ma was unrepentant: only plain language would change people's behaviour. And water use did decrease.

THEATRE IN THE WILDS

In his book *Moving Pictures*, Frederick Arthur Ambrose Talbot, who crossed Canada by rail to report on the potential for settlement, wrote about his visit to Hazelton. He noted that the town was relatively inaccessible, for, when he first visited, the railway was far from completion, and travel was by steamer or dogsled. Nonetheless, a movie man showed up in town and proceeded to open a "theatre." Talbot described the operation:

The operator took over an excavation in the side of the hill overlooking the town, which had been made for storing various goods, but which at that time was empty. In this cramped, unventilated cellar, he rigged his screen and lantern. On the wooden door he nailed a large sheet of paper, on which was scrawled the name of the 'Theatre' and the programme of films 'now being shown.'

The preparations demanded only a few hours. Boxes, barrels, and logs sufficed for seats, while a good many patrons sat or sprawled on the earthen floor. The Indians were amazed and the whites were amused, though the films would not have been tolerated in London or New York, having long since passed their span of usefulness. The show was kept going day after day until the audience became too small to defray the cost of the illuminant, when the 'theatre' was closed, and the showman haunted the verandah of the hotel until he received some new subjects. His supply of films was both uncertain and irregular. He had to order them by post from Vancouver, whence they were brought up by boat. If the fates were kind he received an entire change of programme in about a fortnight; if the river were difficult to navigate, a month passed before they reached him, and often the boat came up without his goods, owing to lack of space. Probably no showman offered to amuse the public under more difficult conditions. It was doubtful if he would secure any films at all during the winter, as, the river being frozen, communication between Hazelton and Prince Rupert had to be maintained by dog trains, which carried letter-mail only.

In comparison with the luxurious conditions under which the triumphs of the art may be seen in London, New York, or Paris, the 'Hazelton Picture Palace' was a half-pathetic half-laughable spectacle—a strange link between civilisation and the aboriginal. I saw it after being immured for several weeks in the primeval bush; and though the pictures in the cellar danced and flickered on the screen, they seemed to me like a welcome handshake with the great world.

Where movies go, censors follow. BC was the first province in Canada to start censoring films. May Watkis, a would-be actress who saw little chance of success in the movies, applied for the job, but it went to a man. She applied to work as his assistant. When the projectionists' union in BC and Washington State refused to teach her the ropes, protesting that she was depriving men of their rightful work, she found a friend to do so, and kept the job.

THIEVES

Diamonds, cash, bonds, even chickens: all these seem reasonable things for a thief to target. But some thieves were of a finer cast of mind, as this letter written to the attorney general from the government agent in Nanaimo in 1889 suggests:

> I have the honor to enclose herein a green silk pocket-handkerchief being the stolen property found in possession of Franklyn—in Reg vs Franklyn whom Mr. Stewart took down to Victoria yesterday to stand his trial for housebreaking . . . I had forgotten to give Mr. Stewart the handkerchief to take to you.

TOOTHSOME

Pioneer settler Tom Leask, who pre-empted land on Quadra Island in 1899, had a double row of teeth, according to Quadra historian Doris Anderson. He liked to pick up a thick beer glass and take a bite out of it—munching several in a row if someone suggested the first had a flaw in it. He may—or may not—have had a bare-fisted battle with a logger all through one night and well into the next day.[9]

TOUGH TIMES

When the going gets tough . . . Back in BC history, with no workers' compensation regulations or help-summoning cellphones, people in the backwoods cultivated a hefty attitude of self-reliance. In December of 1945, the *Alaska Highway News* reported that one Jim Beattie, who had lost a leg while pioneering in the Peace River region, was driving a light delivery truck loaded with fruit that went off a snow-covered road east of Hudson's Hope.

"Though handicapped with the absence of one good leg," the story continued, "Mr. Beattie scrambled up the embankment and walked a mile to Guy Robinson's, where he got a team of horses and a sleigh and then he went back and rescued the fruit."[10]

TRAPPING WHISKERS

On March 6, 1939, the Zeballos *Miner* reported on the success or lack thereof of two trappers who spent the winter of 1939 deep in the north Vancouver Island bush: "Much of the trappers' time was spent making a permanent camp and preparing for next season. They did not get much fur but both came out with prize whiskers."

TREED

Far from the reaches of the conventional law, pioneer townsmen sometimes devised unusual forms of punishment. From the Atlin *Claim*, June 24, 1899:

> In some places dangerous characters are confined in cells. In others, in stocks, but Discovery beats them all in this respect. One individual who was celebrating in a rather boisterous manner....and wetting his whistle

oftener than the law allows was taken in charge by one of Society's brave police on Monday. Having no cells nor stocks for people who transgress the limits of endurance this individual was chained to a tree at the rear of the new court house. There he lay, and there he stood, changing positions as often as the spirit moved. He basked in this bear-like pit for something like seven hours, and the ubiquitous Kodak fiend lost no time in paying homage to so rich a prize; he notified his friend, and then in turn, the friend his friend until the circle was complete with ten of these deadly weapons pointing toward the man. The clock, click, clicks of the kodaks at intervals of a second resembled the discharge of artillery, and as the man changed position and rested against the tree it pictured the acts of the Spaniards before a Cuban prisoner with sentence of death hanging over him. The public finally brought pressure to bear on the authorities to have him removed or liberated. He was liberated.

Chapter Nine
Witchers, Wolverines and Want of Women

UFOS, IFOS

The term "unidentified flying object," or UFO, came into common usage only in the 1950s, but there were many sightings for decades, even centuries, before. The idea that they might signal the presence of people from other planets is relatively new, however; earlier generations were just puzzled by these strange objects.

In 1897, for example, a "fire balloon" appeared repeatedly on the Pacific coast. "What 'it' is, where it comes from or goes to, and who or what manner of men are responsible for its movements, remain just as great a puzzle, however, as when the bright light first made its appearance in the sky," reported the Victoria *Daily Colonist* in August of that year.[1]

On August 6, two Victoria firemen delegated to watch over the remains of a grass fire sighted the object floating low in the sky: "It had no discernible form, balloon shape or otherwise—it was just a great light as large from the distance at which it was viewed as the drum of one of the hose reels, and brighter far... than electric light." The object rose, circled and returned. They rushed to the nearby hotel to find some kind of "night glass," but could get none, returning instead with the night clerk, so he could see the strange light.

A week later, a passenger on the steamer *Rithet* reported he had seen a cigar-shaped object that looked like a bright red star surrounded by a luminous halo travelling slowly through the sky. Another man saw a similar sight through his telescope.

What was it? "The favourite theory seems to be that some daring inventor is trying the product of his brain in the privacy of the night, preparatory to giving his secret to the world." Perhaps it was a mirage; would scientists investigate? Members of the Natural History Society adamantly refused, "being generally of the opinion that there was nothing mysterious about the light seen, but that people had been prepared for something uncanny and consequently felt bound to see it," the *Colonist* continued.

At the same time, there were reports of a mysterious airship seen over Vancouver, and an Indian superintendent reported that several native people had seen a balloon high in the sky headed north over Great Bear Lake. Some suggested this was the balloon flown by Swedish adventurer S.A. Andree, who that summer was trying to fly from Sweden to the North Pole. But by the time the Canadian reports were received, Andree's balloon had crashed, after just two days in the air; he and his party died in their attempts to return to civilization.

VENTRILOQUISTS

The word ventriloquism derives from the Latin for "belly speaker," and refers to a practice that dates back some twenty-five centuries, when some believed that the spirits of the dead migrated to the bellies of prophets, who could foretell the future by having those spirits speak—though why the dead should know about the future is not at all clear. By the end of the 19th century, ventriloquism had lost its prophetic reputation and had become an entertainment, as ventriloquists began to use "dummies"—dolls or figures held by the ventriloquist—who "threw his voice" and seemed to make the dummy speak.

British Columbia had its own homegrown ventriloquist in the 1920s and 1930s. John "Yorkie" Bourke emulated the success of Edgar Bergen and his dummy, Charlie McCarthy—interestingly, made popular through radio, where no one could see the ventriloquist act, but all could appreciate the wisecracks and jokes. Bourke began his entertainment career as a magician. Serving with the Canadian Forces in France during the First World War, Yorkie was called on to do his magic act in a troupe for the troops. He found a discarded ventriloquist's dummy in a box in a theatre, and decided he'd give it a try. He practised for four days, then took his show to the troupe manager. In any classic success story, the manager would have been astonished—and he was, by just how bad Yorkie's act was. Yorkie later reported the manager declared, "as a ventriloquist, you would make a good woodcutter."

But he persevered and improved; he performed for the soldiers, who were impressed. It was the start of a thirty-year career as a ventriloquist, with some 1,800 performances by Yorkie and his dummy, Jerry, in the first twenty years. He had advice for anyone wanting to try it out, but he confessed he hadn't been able to teach anyone the trick. It was, he said, just a gift some people had, though a gift that had to be honed by long and constant practice.[2]

VICE AND DEBAUCHERY

Slow news day? Nothing in particular to editorialize about? Why, then, it was always satisfying to sermonize against debauchery, sin and vices of all kinds. Nineteenth-century newspapermen were not exactly known for their upstanding character, but somehow they saw no hypocrisy is denying the populace what they indulged in themselves. From the Sandon *Paystreak* from December 5, 1896:

> The summary way with which our J.P.'s [Justices of the Peace] are dealing with the tough characters of the city, cannot but meet with the hearty support and commendation of our citizens. There is only one way to deal with the question and that is by adopting a firm and stringent policy of suppression, to the element who gain a livelihood by catering to the devotees of debauchery and vice. There is no lower grade of humanity than this, and if they are allowed to live this parasitical existence the town of Sandon will become nothing more nor less than one huge sink of moral filth. Not only that, but it will become a town in which none of the legitimate trades can prosper on account of the risk of burglary and despoliation which is sure to result if these odds and ends of humanity are not made to either adopt a cleaner and more honest mode of living, or kept moving.

VIGILANTES

Early in gold-rush times, the much-vaunted respect for law 'n' order in BC was fairly hazy, and prospectors, particularly those from the United States, sometimes tried a little vigilante justice. In December of 1858,

Yale saloonkeeper William Foster shot miner Bernard Price. The area magistrate issued a warrant for Foster's arrest and swore in 50 special constables. The following day, two gamblers attacked a black man and beat him "unmercifully."

Aroused by both those crimes, the citizenry called a meeting, and swore to help the magistrate deal with various miscreants, "especially the gamblers and others equally bad then infesting the town."[3]

The gamblers prudently left town. The magistrate shut the gambling houses and revoked their licences. The miners began to talk about lynch law. A constable was rude to the magistrate in court; the magistrate sent the constable to jail. Not more than an hour later, fifteen men—hard cases who had been run out of San Francisco by that city's Vigilance Committee, a vigilante group—returned to Yale and arrested the magistrate in the name of the Queen, while others set the constable free. The magistrate was transported to nearby Hill's Bar, where three men considered corrupt presided over a kangaroo court; they fined the magistrate $50. Seeing no other way out, he paid up. Foster was later reported to have reached Nevada, well distant from the arm of the law or the lynchers. Nothing further was said about the black man.

VOLCANIC BROWN

He was Crazy, he was Volcanic, he was Sunset, he was Doc. Robert Allan Brown got around in the mining regions of BC, acquiring all manner of nicknames: Crazy because he often seemed so; Volcanic because he staked a claim on volcanic rock near Grand Forks and founded Volcanic City; Sunset, for his Sunset Mine; Doc because he acted as a natural healer and, some said, financed his mining ventures by performing backroom abortions.

Whatever the truth of the legends surrounding him, he spent much time in the Boundary Country, showing up there in 1891 and coming and going in the region for some forty years. His Volcanic City, which died aborning, was to embody his beliefs: no banks, churches or schools, which he considered the scourges of modern life, railways coming from all four directions, residents rich and happy in a semi-socialistic utopia.

He had better luck with the claims he staked at Copper Mountain, near Princeton. He sold those for some $42,000, and the mine continued to operate through the 20th century. Brown used part of his payment to buy himself gold false teeth.

In the 1920s, he was drawn to the Pitt Lake region by the legend of Slumach's lost treasure, setting out with only a copy of a letter written by a man who had supposedly found the lode of gold discovered by a native man who was hanged for murder. In 1928, prospecting in the region, Brown was frost-bitten and had to amputate one of his own toes and portions of two more.

He apparently died somewhere near his camp in the Pitt region in the winter of 1930–31, though his body was never found. And neither was Slumach's lost mine.

WAGES OF THIRST

From the Bella Coola *Courier*, November 15, 1913:

A somewhat exciting incident, fortunately attended by no serious results, occurred at Mr. J.M. Rolston's survey camp last Sunday evening.

It appears that Fred Minaty had visited town and returning home in the dark hours became suddenly possessed of a thirst so fierce, that, without waiting to light a lantern, he proceeded to the creek for a pail of water.

Fred says he stumbled over a root, Well, maybe he did.

Wakened, however, by his cries for help, the gang

immediately turned out to find Fred battling for his life in quite two feet of water.

'Tis said the creek is usually quite deep, but then Fred had quite a thirst.

WAITING FOR A LIFT

The lonely life of a lighthouse keeper and his family is well documented: months alone on an island or rocky point, with only the waves for company. And getting ashore for a longed-for visit was rarely easy. One incident appeared in the Port Essington *Sun* on May 18, 1907:

> The trials and tribulations of a lighthouse keeper are numerous enough in the ordinary course of events without the added infliction of disappointment. Mrs. Davis, the wife of the lighthouse keeper on Egg Island, Queen Charlotte Sound, had a novel experience this spring. She had made arrangements in December last to visit in Vancouver in January. When the appointed time came around efforts to secure recognition from passing boats was fruitless. On the approach of a boat Mr. Davis would run up the flag and Mrs. Davis would put on her Sunday clothes. The boats passed on, however. This melancholy procedure went on for three months until the sharp eyes of Capt. Saunders, of the *Camosun*, lit on a small fluttering object at the rear of the fog horn, pulled in and made Mrs. Davis a happy woman.

WAKING WILDLY

Some men sleep more soundly than others, and react more vigorously to being awoken. Nineteen-year-old Atlin prospector Fred Baur found this out to his detriment, and it was almost the last thing he ever discovered.

Baur rose one morning from his miner's tent and cooked his breakfast. The man in the neighbouring tent, Garret Lieniga, was still sleeping soundly. Baur grabbed Lieniga's leg and tried to pull him out of his tent; Lieniga awoke and threatened to shoot Baur if the latter didn't leave him alone. Oh well, thought Baur, he's just feeling cranky this morning.

And he was. A minute later, Lieniga stood in front of Baur's tent, shotgun in hand. Baur tried to dodge out of sight, but Lieniga shot, the charge riddling the right side of Baur's face, with two grains entering his right eye. Baur fell to the ground. Panicky, Lieniga set out to get a doctor.

When Lieniga and the doctor returned, Baur was taken to his tent, where he lay, groaning feebly and taking the occasional sip of water or whisky. Lieniga left once more, supposedly to get more whisky, but took flight instead. He was captured and taken to Atlin. Shortly thereafter, he "became tired of his confinement, and having nothing more than a pair of shackles on his legs, he leisurely sauntered out over the lime swamp."

When the commissioner learned of the escape, "he jumped four feet in the air and gave expression to such sentiments as we positively refuse to publish in this paper." A posse set out to recapture Lieniga.

Fred Baur survived his wounds. Lieniga was not heard of again, though some people thought he might have committed suicide. Baur later described Lieniga, who had helped Baur and his brother carry their vast amounts of supplies into Atlin over the mountain passes, as having a fierce temper, and perhaps slightly demented, since he went off shooting at most unreasonable hours, usually bringing back chipmunks, which he made into stew.⁴

WANT OF WOMEN

What was in shortest supply in gold-rush BC? Not whisky, though certainly men wanted more. Not gold, though they could have done with a little more of that as well. No, what men lamented most was the want of women. A correspondent wrote to the *Times of London* in January of 1862, lamenting the lack:

"Permit me to call attention to a crying evil... viz., the want of women. I believe there is not 1 to every 100 men at the mines; without them the male population will never settle in the country and innumerable evils are the consequence... The miner is not very particular—'plain fat and 50' even would not be objected to; while good-looking girls would be the nuggets and prized accordingly."⁵

Later that year, the first of BC's bride ships arrived. Male Victorians were overjoyed and very curious. "We went aboard the steamer yesterday morning and had a good look at the lady passengers. They are mostly cleanly, well-built, pretty looking young women—ages varying from fourteen to an uncertain figure; a few are young widows who have seen better days. Most appear to have been well raised and generally they seem a superior lot to the women usually met with on emigrant vessels. Taken altogether, we are highly pleased with the appearance of the 'invoice,'" reported the Victoria *Daily Colonist*, "and believe that they will give a good account of themselves in whatever station of life they may be called upon to fill—even if they marry lucky bachelor miners from the Cariboo."[6]

WATER WITCHING

Anyone who has lasted through one of Vancouver Island's wet winters would wonder at the need for a water witcher, a dowser who seeks out water below the surface of the ground. Yet water witchers were indeed in demand, as settlers sought the best place to dig their wells.

One of the best known of the island's dowsers was a small man with a white beard who lived at Seventeen Mile House outside Victoria, and dowsed for water from Sooke to Saanich and beyond. Walter Wrigglesworth, born in 1841, arrived in BC in 1862. He became a firefighter, then chief of the Victoria fire department, then started a cement plant near Seventeen Mile. But he never forgot what he saw while watching a Cariboo miner who was wintering in Victoria as the miner tried to dowse for water. Wrigglesworth tried it himself, and discovered he had the gift.

With his "witchstick"—traditionally a forked hazel or peach tree branch, though he said he could divine with any type of wood—Wrigglesworth located some one hundred and fifty wells in twenty-five years of dowsing, with some water sources as close to the surface as a metre, others thirty metres deep. He said he was not limited to wood, but could also witch for water with lengths of galvanized iron, copper or brass wire twisted into the forked shape, holding wood or wire by the fingertips of both hands and walking over the ground where someone wanted to locate a well.

How did he explain his power? He could not, except to say, "The only reason I can give is that I was born on the stroke of midnight, and so have two birthdays."[7]

Evelyn Penrose didn't need that rationalization. Born in England of a water-divining father who himself had a water-divining mother, Penrose, dramatic and flamboyant, arrived in BC in the 1930s and went to work divining for water, becoming the provincial government's first official water diviner. She later wrote a book detailing her many successes, saying those who dealt with her called her the "Divine Lady."

Penrose claimed to be able to divine not just water, but also gold, oil, illness and even criminal tendencies. Though she usually worked with wood or wire, she tried to develop her abilities to the point where she needed neither. "I stand quite still," she wrote in her autobiography, "stretch out my arm and turn my hand so that the palm and finger tips point outwards and act as a radio receiver. I keep my hand gently moving sideways and backwards and forwards, and turn slowly around. When my hand gets into line with the oil, water or mineral, I immediately feel as if I had a little thread coming out of each finger, connecting me with the deposit. This little thread becomes a string and then a rope and, unless I break the contact by running my left hand down over my arms and fingers, my arm will nearly be pulled out of its socket."[8]

Penrose left BC after a few years, and moved on to Australia.

A WEAKNESS FOR SADDLES

From the Ashcroft *Journal*, May 20, 1916:

Joe Pleo is an Italian by birth and for two years he has been living in and around the vicinity of Lillooet. He apparently has a weakness for saddles, because already having one of his own, he stole another from Mrs. Paul Santini of Lillooet. He removed this during the night, and in his haste, or on account of the darkness, he forgot to take the cinch which seems to have been removed from the saddle. He also forgot to brush away the grey hairs which were sticking in various parts of the saddle. Joe forgot to provide himself with a grey horse for the escapade, and used his own dark colored one. He was arrested on suspicion by Constable Spiller of Clinton, near Kelly lake on May 6th, the day after the disappearance of the saddle. In the witness box the accused said he had bought the saddle from an Indian and had paid $10 for same. He had paid too much, however, he said, as the saddle was only worth $5.00. The cinch was produced in court and in its silent Sherlock Holmes way proved to the jury that the grey horse hairs sticking to itself corresponded to that which were adhering to the saddle. Joe had made no provision against this dumb witness, so he was found guilty. Extenuating circumstances, however, influenced the judge in passing sentence, and he was allowed his liberty.

WHALE OF A TALE

As Robert Service noted, there were strange things done in the midnight sun, but there were even more strange things seen in the ocean's sheen off the coast of BC. (See *Sea Serpents*, page 171, for other examples.) Some of the amazing creatures and events reported along the coast were more myth or legend than reality. But occasionally, the strangeness was real. In 1920, scientists and onlookers were fascinated by reports that a whale with hind legs, the first ever discovered, had been brought in to the Kyuquot whaling station. The *New York Times* and newspapers around the United States were agog at the discovery.

The whale was captured in July 1919, off the west coast of Vancouver Island. Two hind "legs" protruded from the animal's underside. Officials of the whaling station sent one of the legs to the provincial museum; the crew apparently kept the other as a souvenir. The museum's preserved leg bones were sent on to the American Museum of Natural History, where they were exhaustively studied by scientists who concluded they were indeed vestigial limbs. In later days, the whale and her limbs have been cited as evidence for evolution, a reminder of the days when whale-like creatures walked upon the land. On November 9, 1920, the *New York Times* reported:

The first whale with hind legs ever discovered by man has been caught at a whaling station near British Columbia, it was announced in a lecture at the Natural History Museum last evening. The bones of one of the legs were shown to the audience, who were told that as far as scientists know a whale thus equipped has never before been seen ... The legs projected some four feet from the body near the tail, and were about six inches broad, the bones being covered with a thick layer of blubber which may or may not have contained muscle. The whale, a female fifty feet in length, was unfortunately not preserved at the Victoria whaling station.

WHISKY WATERED

Rye whisky, rye whisky, rye whisky, they cried—quite frequently in Prohibition years. But, sadly, sometimes it was not. From the Prince George *Citizen*, February 5, 1911:

Two Prince Rupert women who paid a stranger $1480 in cash for one excellent whisky feel that they have a grievance. The women thought they were buying for this money 45 gallons of the forbidden intoxicant, and the test they made convinced them that the quality was good. Later they discovered that a capsule containing about a pint of liquor had been fitted under the bung and that the remainder of the barrel was full of water. The man having disposed of the lonely pint at a rate of $11,380 a gallon, which undoubtedly constitutes a record, left for the south and is believed to be in Vancouver.

WIVES WONDERING

Many men came west, leaving their wives and children behind and promising to send for them—or at least send money for them—as soon as they was able. It didn't always happen: men frequently disappeared and were never heard of again by their families. Some were undoubtedly killed, but the majority, it would seem, decided to stay AWOL. The McBride *Journal* of December 17, 1914, told one such tale:

> There was a lady in our office this morning claiming to be the wife of Mr. G.B. Watson. She said that the last time she heard of him he was somewheres in the north working as a civil engineer on one of the railroads . . . She said he is a man about 35 years old, about 6 ft. 2 in. in height.
> The lady seemed to be in destitute circumstance and was very anxious to locate her husband.

WOLF SEES THE LIGHT

While most of the "beast attacks man" stories in BC have to do with bears, occasionally a wolf or a cougar was the culprit. Railway signalman Fred Hines found a novel way of dealing with a wolf, reported in the McBride *Journal* on December 17, 1914:

> When Fred Hines was on duty in the west yard on Tuesday night, he did some great signaling work, giving the engineer on the yard engine highballs and signs of all kinds that were not provided for in the code. On the arrival of Mr. Pedlar on the engine, he found that Mr. Hines had been attacked by a large timber wolf, and had been defending himself with his lantern swinging it

round and round in the wolf's face as the animal circled round him growling and snapping. The approach of the engine frightened the wolf away.

WOLVERINE WHIMSY

The animals of wild BC fascinated visitors. The less known they were to a writer's potential readers, the more they warranted a story or two. From *BC 1887, A Ramble in British Columbia*:

> This animal [the wolverine], it appears, is so suspicious of the schemes of its enemies that the only way to catch it is to put a trap without any bait or concealment in the unlikeliest place for it to come. Then lay any amount of snares, and lures, and cunningly concealed ambushes everywhere else. The wolverine will be so awfully pleased with his own smartness in detecting and avoiding these devices that he will march straight into the one prepared for him.
>
> One we were told of which came down a chimney and played the common or garden fool in a man's hut. He was going away for a few days, so set a heavy trap in the fireplace, which, however, he omitted to secure. A neighbour

next day hearing diabolical noises in the hut, went and peeped through a chink in the door, and there saw what he supposed to be the Devil, a fearsome being all glaring eyes and shaggy hair. The house appeared to have had a company of fiends playing Rugby football in it, if one could imagine demons so devoid of common sense as to engage in that pastime. Everything movable was smashed and torn into flinders, and the whole place, including his Satanic majesty, covered thickly with flour. The discoverer, being a courageous man, commenced shooting at the infernal visitant through the chinks, and at last succeeded in killing him; and then the door being opened a wolverene with a steel trap on his leg was disclosed to view, the general jamboree in which everything was embraced being the result of the owner's carelessness in leaving the trap unfastened. There was not one single thing, it was said, left in that cabin that had not been smashed, upset, or rent in pieces by the infuriated animal in its efforts to escape, the trap being too heavy for it to return up the chimney.

WOMEN'S RIGHTS—OR MAYBE LEFTS

Don't talk to strange men, runs the rule we tell our children now. But a strange man talking to women might pay a heavy penalty in earlier days. From the Rossland *Miner*, July 29, 1899:

> One of the most estimable married women in Rossland, who, however, is not in a position to occupy a residence where she can cook as she would like to, tried a new restaurant yesterday and came out and started for home. Her charms seemed to affect the sensibilities of a well-dressed middle-aged man, who immediately tried to launch a flirtation with her. Before leaving for lunch, however, her husband had asked her to call for a hammer and when the wretch asked, "Where are you living now, dear?" she struck him with the hammer in the mouth with such force that he will probably have to go to the dentist for repairs.

WORK AND WAGES

Chinese immigrants to BC were often portrayed as being clannish, secretive and loyal each to each regardless of circumstance. But that wasn't always the case. In 1891, six who termed themselves "subjects of the Chinese Empire" petitioned the attorney general of BC for help. "Through being stupid and inexperienced, [we] have been taken advantage of," they wrote, in Chinese, and asked that the Justice of the Peace in the Kootenay area be instructed to pay them the money collected from one Chu Kee or Ah Kee, who had tried to disappear without paying his debts.

"All are aware that gain should be obtained righteously and that when clearly it has not been righteously obtained, it causes unrest in the common people," they declared. Chu Kee had, in fact been arrested; officials confiscated $400 from him. Chu Kee was then set free, on condition that he would forfeit the money to the petitioners if he did not return. He did not come back, so, asked the men, could they now get their money? They had been told the money would go to the government, but that seemed most unfair. "Does it not seem as if because we are stupid and inexperienced, that therefore we can be imposed on?"[9]

The response of the attorney general is not recorded.

WRESTLEMANIA

Wrestling matches were a highlight of life in the backwoods, with travelling wrestlers coming to town to perform—and sometimes to take on all comers. "No holds barred," was a true description of the old-time matches. On October 17, 1888, the Victoria *Daily Colonist* reported on a match in Vancouver:

> The wrestling match at Vancouver on Saturday night between D. Cameron of Victoria, and Richardson of Winnipeg, was awarded to the latter. Cameron won the first fall, and in the second bout, when the men were struggling, a lamp fell and broke. Cameron wanted to quit, as the broken glass was cutting him. But Richardson having the advantage would not give up. The referee refused to interfere, and when the men were finally separated both were terribly cut, Cameron especially. In the third round Cameron was too terribly cut to proceed and the referee awarded the match to Richardson. Great dissatisfaction was manifested and Cameron entered a protest.

Over in Rossland, an announcement of an upcoming wrestling match followed closely on a description of a meeting at the tabernacle the previous night, on the subject of the second coming of the lord in the clouds of Heaven:

"Hali Aldai, the Sultan's lion, will wrestle Al Tobakine, the champion of London and Paris tonight... Each has wagered $200 on the result. Hali Aldai agrees to throw Tobakine three times in 40 minutes... William Zepp and Frank Fraser will wrestle with the Turk and he promises them $1 a minute as long as they are able to prevent themselves from being thrown.[10]

Famed newspaper editor Ma Murray wrote some of the best descriptions, retailing the stories of scissorholds and half-nelsons with verve and passion. One such tale appeared in the Bridge River-Lillooet *News* on April 7, 1934:

> Plenty of nerve-tingling action, the odd display of temper and enough real wrestling skill to draw almost continuous roars of applause from the crowd of 1,500 marked the weekly mat show in Vancouver Thursday night.
> Ted Thye of Portland, odds-on favorite to beat the Arizona Navajo Chief Little Wolf, didn't disappoint his backers, though his displays of temper and his fondness

for the refuge of the ropes whenever the going got tough, didn't endear him to the fans.

Ted softened the Redman with several lusty shoulder blows to pin him in the first canto. The Navajo fought grimly and in the fourth clamped on his dreaded "Indian Deathlock." Thye held out for only a few seconds, then came up raging and lusting for Indian gore...

Jack Forsgren and Marvin Westenberg slugged, scowled and struggled mightily through three rounds to a no-fall draw.

She wrote another for the Bridge River-Lillooet *News* of May 23, 1934:

Just when Jack Forsgren, Vancouver Fireman, and everyone else in the big arena thought Jack "Texas" League was softened to the point where all that was necessary was for Forsgren to fall on him to win the match, the former Texas boxer came to and hung a cruel haymaker on the Forsgren chin for a knockout and victory... Howard Cantonwine tired of trying to make veteran John Freberg turn savage and nearly strangled the ancient Swede with the notorious hangman's trick.

YANKEES, DAMNED AND OTHERWISE

Americans, yes; Americans, no. In the early days of the colony of BC, there were probably more Americans than Britons or Canadians flocking to the gold-bearing rivers and rocks. This was good or bad, depending on your point of view. If you read the *Times* of London or the Toronto *Globe*, it was a dreadful state of affairs, with the bumptious and presumptuous Yankees extraordinarily annoying. If you were American, the American presence was an excellent thing. The border between the two regions had been set in 1848, but from the late 1850s into the 1870s when BC finally joined Canadian Confederation, there was a considerable body of opinion that the region should become part of the United States, and speeches were made in the US Congress putting that view forward with great vigour.

Surveyor Charles Wilson had much to do with Americans as he travelled the border between the regions in 1858 and 1859. He was not particularly taken with the American incomers. "Yankees certainly are the most provoking men to have anything to do with, you can never get a decisive answer out of them," he wrote in his diary in October of 1858, as he suffered through endless rain at Fort Langley.[11]

John Nugent, in 1858 the special agent of the US in Victoria, saw it differently, finding his fellow citizens rather fine—though he might have discovered few such paragons had he ventured up-country to the gold-rush sites:

"The sobriety of their deportment, their decent observance of all the proprieties of life, in the midst of privations and annoyances of no common degree, and their obedience to the law under very trying provocations to its infringement, although they may not have gained for them such liberal treatment as was due to that forebearance and good conduct, have, nonetheless, commanded the respect of the strangers among whom they are cast, and cannot fail to be subjects of pride and gratulation to their own Government... The forebearance... of the citizens of the United States, their quiet observation of the laws under any aggressions on their rights of which they may have to complain, will not alone have its reward in the consciousness of having done credit to their country—a country whose institutions are based upon that all-pervading love of order and that spirit of obedience to the law which distinguishes its citizens—but it will moreover, entitle them to the active intervention of their own government for the redress of their grievances and for the protection of their rights."[12]

But the correspondent for the *Times* was not convinced. "The Americans did not count the cost of insulting or attacking us," he wrote in September of 1859, as the celebrated Pig War (see page 155) broke out over the killing of a pig on San Juan Island. "They forgot their old enemies the Indians, who are burning with revenge, thirsting for their blood. Let it once be known that the English are no longer friendly with the Americans, and slumbering feuds will break out; but let it be known that they are at war, and 100,000 Indians will attack the Americans unasked... The news from the mines very good."

ZANARDI ZEALOUSNESS

Write about this province long enough, and one day, a caller will phone or someone will write to declare that he or she is related to royalty—perhaps even a by-blow of Edward VIII, a noted man-about-town who visited Canada in 1919 as Prince of Wales—and the claimant is eager to submit to blood tests to prove the relationship. Or you'll find in some out-of-the-way hamlet a grizzled loner with week-old egg in his beard who, townsfolk will whisper to you, is actually the long-lost Count of Upper Slobovia.

Truth is, however, a number of royal relations and/or royal pretenders did make their way to BC, some of them the black-sheep sons of famous families, some of them adventure seekers, some of them younger sons of impoverished nobility trying to improve their lot. One of the more interesting claimants was Caroline Zanardi Landi, wife of the five-foot-tall Count Zanardi Landi. The latter was said to have arrived in BC from Smyrna, then Greek but now the Turkish city of Izmir, in 1906 "without any money but with a large selection of sporting guns." He told people in Prince Rupert he had had to flee Europe because he had married a niece of Empress Elizabeth, wife of Franz Joseph, Emperor of Austro-Hungary. In truth, he married Caroline Zuhnelt in Vancouver, and adopted her two children by a previous marriage. He worked on railway construction out of Prince Rupert; a nearby bridge and rapids bear his name.

Caroline claimed in a long book about her life to have been the secret daughter of the Empress. She didn't name her father, but some suggest he might have been a Hungarian nobleman. In any case, Caroline and the count returned to Europe in about 1911, and the lady pressed her claim with no apparent result. Her daughter, Elissa Landi, became a movie actress, starring opposite such leading men as Ronald Coleman.

Endnotes

Chapter One: Anarchists, Bawdy Houses, Bullets, Buttocks and Bears
1. *New York Times*, October 10, 1911.
2. Victoria *Daily Colonist*, October 10, 1911.
3. Victoria *Daily Colonist*, December 8, 1911.
4. As quoted in *The Skeena, River of Destiny*, p. 128.
5. *The Skeena, River of Destiny*, p. 42–43.
6. As recounted in *Columbia River Chronicles*, p. 46.
7. As quoted in *The Skeena, River of Destiny*, p. 166.

Chapter Two: Camels, Communists, Duels and Desperados
1. Victoria *Daily British Colonist*, March 1, 1862.
2. Victoria *Daily British Colonist*, May 3, 1862.
3. "Cariboo," Vancouver *Province*, 1895, as quoted in *Pioneer Days in British Columbia, Volume 2*.
4. *BC 1887, A Ramble in British Columbia*, p. 293–94.
5. *Klondike Cattle Drive*, p. 4, p. 6.
6. Victoria *Daily British Colonist*, June 4, 1871.
7. Victoria *Daily Colonist*, November 18, 2002.
8. Victoria *Daily Colonist*, October 9, 1896.
9. *Cannery Village, Company Town*, p. 250–51.

Chapter Three: Elephants, Editors and Flim-Flam Men
1. Columbia Basin Institute of Regional History, www.basininstitute.org/home/elephant/main_event.html
2. August 20, 1909.
3. *Whitewater Men of the Skeena*, p. 12.
4. Victoria *Daily Colonist*, October 12, 1894.
5. Sandon *Paystreak*, October 13, 1900.
6. Port Essington *Sun*, August 17, 1907.

Chapter Four: Hangmen, Highwaymen, Horses and Hens
1. Attorney General files 200/95, BC Archives.
2. Victoria *Daily Colonist*, March 24, 1893.
3. Victoria *Daily Colonist*, June 8, 1894.
4. Victoria *Daily Colonist*, November 8, 1885.
5. Chilliwack *Free Press*, October 18, 1912.
6. *Maclean's* magazine, September 1, 1922, p. 46.
7. Prince George *Citizen*, July 30, 1918.

Chapter Five: Loathsome, Lulu, Madness and Moose
1. Prince Rupert *News*, June 3, 1911.
2. http://freepages.genealogy.rootsweb.ancestry.com/~jtenlen/ORBios/bonser.txt
3. May 31, 1899.
4. Wilmer, *Canterbury Outcrop*, July 10, 1902.
5. *Mapping the Frontier*, p. 49.
6. *Mapping the Frontier*, p. 63.
7. *BC 1887, A Ramble in British Columbia*, p. 82.

Chapter Six: Necromancers, Opium Smugglers and Not Dead Yet
1. Victoria *Daily Colonist*, December 11, 1873.
2. Victoria *Daily Colonist*, May 31, 1892.
3. *"Spiritualism," or, Modern necromancy: a sermon with preface and notes* (Victoria), 1870.
4. Victoria *Daily Colonist*, June 2, 1891.
5. Victoria *Daily Colonist*, October 23, 1897.
6. Ms. in the collection of the Jasper Yellowhead Museum and Archives.
7. As quoted in the *Kootenay Mail*, June 23, 1894.
8. *The Skeena, River of Destiny*, p. 142.
9. *New York Times*, December 22, 1888.

Chapter Seven: Pigs, Potatoes and Pills for All Ills
1. Attorney General files 166/72, BC Archives.
2. Prince George *Citizen*, January 28, 1919.

3. Prince George *Citizen*, February 15, 1919.
4. Rossland *Miner*, August 31, 1899.
5. Queen Charlotte *Islander*, October 2, 1911.

Chapter Eight: Sea Serpents, Suicides and Theatre in the Wilds
1. July 17, 1890.
2. April 16, 1919.
3. *Daily British Colonist*, December 28, 1870.
4. *Whitewater Men of the Skeena*, p. 9–10.
5. Atlin *Claim*, May 6, 1899.
6. Attorney General files 60/80, BC Archives.
7. *The Skeena, River of Destiny*, p. 144.
8. As quoted in *Ma Murray and the Newspapering Murrays*, by Georgina Keddell, p. 290.
9. *Evergreen Islands: a History of the Islands of the Inside Passage*, p. 21.
10. *Alaska Highway News*, December 13, 1945.

Chapter Nine: Witchers, Wolverines and Want of Women
1. Victoria *Daily Colonist*, August 7, 1897.
2. Victoria *Daily Times*, November 19, 1938.
3. Victoria *British Colonist*, January 8, 1859.
4. Atlin *Claim*, May 6 and May 13, 1899.
5. *The Times* of London, January 13, 1862.
6. Victoria *Daily Colonist*, September 19, 1862.
7. Victoria *Daily Colonist*, June 5, 1910.
8. *Adventure Unlimited*, p. 94.
9. Attorney General files 599/91, BC Archives.
10. Rossland *Miner*, August 5, 1899.
11. *Mapping the Frontier*, p. 37.
12. *The Times* of London, January 19, 1859.

Bibliography

Many books, newspapers and original sources were consulted in the writing of this book. Among the books listed below are those referred to in the endnotes.

Adventure Unlimited: A Water Diviner Travels the World, by Evelyn Penrose (London: Neville Spearman, 1958).

BC 1887, A Ramble in British Columbia, by J.A. Lees and W. J. Clutterbuck (London: Longmans, Green, and Co., 1888).

Cannery Village, Company Town, by K. Mack Campbell (Victoria: Trafford, 2004).

Columbia River Chronicles: a history of the Kootenay district in the 19th century, by B.R. Atkins, E. L. Affleck, G. B. Forde (Vancouver: Nicolls Press, 1976).

Evergreen Islands: a History of the Islands of the Inside Passage, by Doris Anderson (Sidney: Gray's Publishing, 1979).

Klondike Cattle Drive, by Norman Lee (Vancouver: Mitchell Press, 1960).

Ma Murray and the Newspapering Murrays, by Georgina Keddell (Halifax: Goodread Biographies, 1984).

Mapping the Frontier, George F.G. Stanley, ed. (Toronto: Macmillan of Canada, 1970).

Moving Pictures, by Frederick Arthur Ambrose Talbot (London: Heinemann, 1912).

Pioneer Days in British Columbia, Volume 2, Art Downs, ed. (Surrey: Heritage House, 1979).

The Skeena, River of Destiny, by R.G. Large (Vancouver: Mitchell Press, 1957).

Vagabond Verses, by Crosbie Garstin (London: Sidgwick & Jackson, Ltd., 1917).

Whitewater Men of the Skeena, by Wiggs O'Neill (Kitimat, BC: Northern Sentinel Press, 1960).

Index

#
150 Mile House, 98
70 Mile House, 174

A
Aldergrove, 46
Americans, bad and good, 217
Anderson, James, versifier, 43
Anyox, 143
Ashnola John, duellist, 51
Ashcroft, 93, 208
Atlin, 85, 96, 121, 157, 173, 180, 204
Austrians, mad, 118

B
Baur, Fred, prospector, 204
Beacon Hill Park, 51
Bedaux, Charles, entrepreneur, quixotic, 138–40
Bella Coola, 175, 202
Bennett, 97
Bulkley Valley, 71
Bosco, necromancer, 136
Boston Bar, 70
Bourke, John "Yorkie," ventriloquist, 198
Boyd, William, shot by a gun on the floor, 174
Bridge River, 70, 187
Brown, Robert Allan (Crazy, Volcanic, Sunset, Doc), 201
Burns, Thomas, jail escape artist, 66
Burdock Blood Bitters, 150
Burns, William, Kanaka groom, 6
Burton, 73, 101
Butts, John, malingerer, 25

C
Campbell, K. Mack, canneries historian, 49
Canals, 123
Cary, George Hunter, attorney general and eccentric, 50
Caux, Jean Jacques (Cataline), packer, 36
Charlie Ed, escapist elephant, 62
Charlie Lake, 45
Chila, 76
Chilliwack, 104, 130, 147, 159, 166, 171
Clutterbuck, W.J., and Lees, J.A., authors/travellers, 24, 131
Coleman, Kitty, madam, 150
Columbia River, 123
Cortes Island, 150
Counterfeiting, 8–9, 41
Cowichan, 108
Cranbrook, 61–64
Creston, 123
Cridge, Bishop Edward, moralist, 137
Cutlar, Lyman, Pig War catalyst, 155

D
D'Arcy Island, 112
Discovery, punishment in, 193
Dupen, James, would-be hangman, 90
Durant, Captain Harry, opium smuggler, 145

E

Egg Island lighthouse, 203
Embree, Alexander and Walter, bear fighters, 21–22

F

fighting, women, 6–7
Flood, Charley, everyone knows, 81
Fort St. John, 140, 187
Fraser Valley, 130

G

Gates, Swiftwater Bill, marrying man, 124–25
Giscome, 105
Golden, 129, 154
Graham Island, 163
Grand Trunk Pacific, 156
Greenwood, 116
Griffin Charles, Pig War combatant, 155
Grohman, William Adolph Baillie, canal builder and failed visionary, 123–24

H

Hazelton, 36–38, 113; movies in, 189–90
Herrmann the Great, necromancer, 137–38
Higgins, D.W., storyteller, 52
Hogan, Lew, (Jr.), cannery worker, 49
Howe Sound, monsters in, 171
Hudson's Hope, 192

I

Israelowitz, Adolph, embezzler, 65

J

Joslyn, C.J. (Boss Harris), shadowy opium smuggler, 144

K

Kalskino Inlet, dynamite suicide, 181
Kamloops, 42, 50, 91, 129
Kansas Kid, 110, 112
Kaslo, 116
Kelly, Bulldog, murderer, 24–25
Kennedy, Michael, possible paramour slayer, 129
Kergan, John, Trial Island hermit, 94–95
Kitselas Canyon, 15, 71
Kootenay River, 123
Kyuquot, walking whale found, 209

L

Ladner, potatoes in, 159
Ladysmith, 83
Langstaff, J.J., newspaper editor, 33
Leask, Tom, too many teeth, 192
Lee, Norman, cattle driver, 37–38
Leechtown, Spaniards and lost mine in, 152
Leon, Albert, anarchist counterfeiter, 8–10
Lieniga, Garret, cranky in the mornings, 204
Lillooet, route to goldfields, 31
Lorne Creek, spirits help finding gold near, 179
Lowery, Colonel Robert Thornton, newspaper editor, 2, 59, 79, 99, 115–16, 143

M

Marble, Charles, failed balloonist, 75
Massett, 163
Maynard, Hannah, photographer and spiritualist, 137
McBride, 61, 211; fighting wolves in, 211
Mission City, 118
monsters, of various types, 172 ff.
Montagneuse, 77
Moricetown, 103
movies, 190–91
Murray, Margaret (Ma), newspaper editor, 2, 59, 187–88, 216

N

Nakusp, 73, 116
Nanaimo, 11, 41, 117, 192
Naramata, 138
Nelson, 47, 66, 73, 119
New Denver, 116, 117
Nootka Island, 8, 9

O

O'Neill, Wiggs, raconteur, 15
Ocean Falls, 175
Okanagan, 31, 51, 84, 138
opium, smuggling, 144–45

P

Peace River, 76, 140, 192
Penrose, Evelyn, water dowser, 207
Phoenix, 59-60, 81, 101
Pine City, suicide in, 180
Pleo, Joe, saddle aficionado, 208
Port Essington, 23, 79, 80, 170
Port Simpson, 170
Portland Canal, 57, 60, 86, 122

Pouce Coupe, 35, 141
Prince Rupert, 14, 15, 52, 68, 102, 118, 143, 173, 175, 186, 191, 220; watered whisky in, 210

Q

Quadra Island, 192
Queen Charlotte City, 163
Queen Charlotte Islands, 90
Quesnel, 146
Quin Que, hen owner, 93

R

Radcliffe, J.R., hangman, 90–91
Ramsey, Bruce, historian. 32
Redgrave, Stephen, BC doubter, 186
Revelstoke, 154
Robinson, Charles Moore, developer and believer in the beyond, 138
Rossland, 33, 66, 81, 158, 216; honourable women in, 214

S

Salmon Arm, 56
Sandon, 16, 34, 78, 79, 99, 199
Seventeen Mile House, 206
Similkameen, 151
Skeena River, 15, 37, 38, 71, 73, 113, 179
Solberg, Minnie and Bergilot, cougar ladies, 40–41
Spaniards, in BC, 151–52
Squamish, 146
Stevenson, Robert, duellist, 51
Stewart, 57, 122, 178
Stikine, 30, 119, 139, 141
Surprise, 185
Sweet, Lulu, 115

T

Talbot, Frederick Arthur Ambrose, movie historian, 189–90
Tlell River, 163
Trail, 59, 66
Trial Island, 94
Trout Lake, 141

U

Upper Arrow Lake, monsters in, 172

V

Vancouver, bank robbers in, 161; wrestling in, 215
Victoria, Communists in, 39; day in court, 12; morgue, 129; opium in, 144–46; rogues and vagabonds in, 165; UFOs over, 196

W

Wells, 3, 16
Wilby, Ralph, embezzler, 64–65
Wilby, Thomas, long-distance driver, 103
Wilson, Charles, surveyor and mosquito-hater, 130–31
Wilson, Eva, soiled dove, 125
Wrigglesworth, Walter, water dowser, 206

Y

Yale, 7, 56, 127, 200

Z

Zanardi Landi, Caroline and Count, 219–20
Zeballos, 17, 35, 69, 126, 162

Acknowledgments

The basis for this book is the material produced by the story tellers of Canada's west coast: the writers of letters, books, newspaper articles, magazine pieces and all the other sources that make up the unofficial history of daily life in British Columbia. Without their ear for a tall tale, their love of the unusual and their recognition of the bizarre, the written history of this province might be limited to politics, economics and official records. I am in their debt.

I thank also Ruth Linka at TouchWood Editions, for her support; Marlyn Horsdal, my editor, for the exercise of her editing skills and for her long-time friendship; and my partner, Joe Thompson, with whom I share not only a life but also a love of the offbeat and the absurd.

Rosemary Neering has been writing about British Columbia for more than thirty years, always seeking out the unusual and quirky tales that abound in this province's history. The author of *Wild West Women: Travellers, Adventurers and Rebels*, *Down the Road: Journeys Through Small-Town British Columbia* and *A Traveller's Guide to Historic British Columbia*, as well as a number of other works on BC and Canadian history, she has written prolifically for publications such as *British Columbia* magazine. When she isn't skulking down archival alleyways, you can find Rosemary in Victoria, where she lives with her partner, Joe Thompson, and her cat. She gardens, creates hand-built pottery, and plays tennis and pickleball.